Marnie's Kitchen Shortcuts

Marnie's Kitchen Shortcuts

MARNIE SWEDBERG

ST. MARTIN'S GRIFFIN/NEW YORK

NOTE: Pricing information was collected in the Upper Midwest between 1993 and 1994. Please consider that prices vary from place to place and that they are always on the rise.

MARNIE'S KITCHEN SHORTCUTS. Copyright © 1996 by Marnie Swedberg. Illustrations copyright © 1996 by Durell Godfrey. All rights reserved. Printed in the United States of America. No part of this book may be used or reproduced in any manner whatsoever without written permission except in the case of brief quotations embodied in critical articles or reviews. For information, address St. Martin's Press, 175 Fifth Avenue, New York, N.Y. 10010

Book design by Gretchen Achilles

Library of Congress Cataloging-in-Publication Data

Swedberg, Marnie.
  Marnie's kitchen shortcuts / by Marnie Swedberg.
     p.   cm.
  Includes bibliographical references and index.
  ISBN 0-312-14119-X
  1. Cookery.   I. Title.
TX651.S93   1996
641.5—dc20   95-45073
                                              CIP

First St. Martin's Griffin Edition: June 1996
10   9   8   7   6   5   4   3   2   1

This book is dedicated to my husband, Dave, for making it possible for me to pursue my dreams, and to Mark, Keren, and Timothy, the best kids a mom could ever hope for.

This book is also dedicated to my *Amah-El* girls (Hebrew for Servant Girl of the Lord):
Wendy Jensen, Sarah Daniels, Rachel Orvis, Michelle Helweg, Ruth Heppner, Hannah Karwoski, Kacie Hecker, Ronda Heppner, Melissa Pratt, Amanda Heppner, Betsy Blanshan, Carrie Blanshan, Janelle Tessier, Kari Harder, Jennifer Lewis, Brandi Fish, Sheena Estling, Stephanie Brekke, Bridgette Baus, Chelsea Boekelheide, Bethany Lisell, Amanda Patch, Amy Hegstad, Amber Schwab, Jana Knight, Jenny Lee, Amy Sadoski, Kristen Yanok, Sarah Peterson, and Tabby Hamilton.

Contents

Acknowledgments

Thank you, Dad and Mom, for introducing me to my Heavenly Father and for instilling in me the confidence to face new challenges and to benefit from past failures.

Thank you, Irv and Doris, for your wholehearted love and encouragement.

Thank you, dear friends and proofreaders: Vicki Foster, Nancy Fisher, and Michelle Ortmann.

Thank you, Mary Casanova, Aggie Hollarah, and Muriel Nelson, for the technical help. Thank you, Barb Larson and Merle Pratt, for research assistance.

Thank you, Barbara Anderson, for seeing merit in my work and for committing your talents to the job of bringing it to publication.

Additional thanks to Marla Hartson, Lynnette Danielson, Deb Swedberg, Carolyn Karwoski, Karen Fausher, Gwynn Conrad, Sandy Ellerbusch, Tammy Milbrath, Susan Helweg, Tammy Myrick, Connie Bulow, Marcia Mehlhaff, Joni Larrieu, Marie Colwill, Melody Unruh, Mary Daniels, Tanya Dorholt, Lynne Hartzell, Katy Ellerbusch, Mindy Eklund, Tami Russell, Nancy Peterson, Rosie Orvis, JuNell Caravetta, and everyone else who helped with ideas and recipe testing.

Marnie's Kitchen Shortcuts

1.

Introduction to Savings

Time flies, weight climbs, and money vanishes into thin air. A number of years ago my husband, Dave, designed and built a 120-gallon aquarium. It was beautiful, but it began to leak and there was no sign of trouble until water had soaked through the carpet and floor, and we noticed it dripping from the basement ceiling tiles. Once we knew there was a leak, we quickly located the source and sealed it before further damage was done, but I shudder to think what might have happened if we hadn't noticed those soggy ceiling tiles.

In a similar way, your time, money, and health may be needlessly trickling away and you may not even realize it until something serious goes wrong. This book takes less than two hours to read and offers you the ability to spot the source of those leaks and seal them without spending a fortune or wasting a lot of time. In fact, the following pages include everything you need to know to prepare nutritious meals for a fraction of the cost during time you would have spent cooking from boxes or waiting in fast-food lines for expensive, greasy burgers.

When first married, I had time to prepare meals from scratch and we enjoyed good food at reasonable prices. But as children appeared on the scene and life got busier, I found myself relying more on prepackaged foods and I watched in horror as our food spending mushroomed to nearly three times what it had been. Even with a background in management, I felt almost helpless to stop the upward spiral. I had no time for cooking, no money for convenience foods, and no pride in what I was serving.

My stress level seemed to rise right along with our food costs. Our family had so many conflicting needs. We were determined to live on one income, yet I was not willing to spend my life hugging the stove. We wanted to entertain, but the meals our budget could handle were nothing we wanted to serve to guests. Furthermore, National Merit Society Studies had proven that shared family mealtimes led to high-achieving kids and to increased stability in marriage and improvements in work performance.

My traditional approach to food shopping, meal planning, and food preparation was not working, so I set out to find and stop the leaks. I began to search for quicker and easier ways to do things, and I came across ideas that saved a little time here and a few dollars there. As I began to apply new strategies I discovered a freedom I had only dreamed of.

Today our food bill is lower than it was six years ago, in spite of inflation and the fact that our family is larger and we share meals with fifty to seventy-five guests each month. These are attractive, *balanced meals* including a main dish, side dishes, and dessert. I spend less than 50¢ per person per meal on food, and I *never* serve cabbage stews, bean casseroles, or anything else that would trigger thoughts of a penny-pinching host.

And, thankfully, the days of slaving for savings are gone: I sometimes arrive in the kitchen less than fifteen minutes before a meal is to be served and actually pull it off. I never waste time on midweek trips to the grocery store to pick up missing meal components; everything I need is already here. I enjoy savings of up to 80 percent by using small snatches of time to make my own dry mixes, and my freezer is full of homemade convenience options that I made with time I was going to spend at the stove anyway.

Every person is different and every family has different needs, but if you read this book, you will find yourself spending less on food—and less time in the kitchen. You'll realize immediate savings by making even a few small changes, and you will see your savings continue as you incorporate more of the concepts into your family's routine.

Government statistics estimate that the average American spends $32.69 per week on food. You have your own best interest at heart when you decide to manage your food spending instead of letting *it* manage *you*. Taking control means finding—and stopping—the leaks, and it's my goal in this book to help make you aware of the potential trouble spots and to provide strategies for fixing or eliminating them. We'll focus on *quick fixes* (did you know that by eliminating just one midweek trip to the grocery store you can save up to an hour in travel, parking, shopping, and storage time, and as much as $25 on the food itself?), *organizational strategies* (pantry and kitchen setup, for example), and *long-term solutions* (such as monthly meal planning that includes family and guests) to get you back in control of your food, time, and calorie budgets.

Each of our lives and households and families is unique, but it seems universal that we all need more time and more money to pursue our individual goals. I've found that it's in the kitchen that great gains can be made in a family's finances and fun time, and I've assembled these kitchen shortcuts—tips, hints, strategies, and solutions that have worked for me—to help you achieve all that you want out of life.

2.

Small Changes That Can Lead to Big Results

When supper time rolls around and ideas or energy for dinner preparation are long since spent, it matters little if you are an at-home mom, a nanny whose responsibilities include child care and cooking, or a professional on your way home from work. Being a creative and caring chef is a triumph on a good day and a tragedy on a bad one.

Through the years, quality home cooking has given way to fast foods, boxed side dishes, prepackaged mixes, and frozen dinner combinations. Advertising rhetoric assures us that this is the best we can hope for and when it's the 175th meal of *this year* that needs to be made, we aren't in any mood to argue.

Fortunately, feeding your family nurturing foods on a consistent basis is within reach. Stress can be replaced with simplicity; the eating frenzy with eye-to-eye communication; and expensive, empty calories with delicious, nutritious, and inexpensive entrées.

While financial and nutritive considerations are important, our first priority will be to reduce the stress caused by the never-ending pressure to plan, prepare, and present yet another pleasing meal.

The Kitchen Notebook

Efficient time and money management is key to success in the business world and there is much to be gained by bringing these same strategies home. As the appointment book is to the professional, so the Kitchen Notebook is to the person responsible for meal planning and execution.

If I were to teach a course in home food management, I'd start with the analogy of a person who buys one gallon of gas at a time. We'd all agree that this person would be better off to save up and buy at least a half tank of gas at each station visit instead of wasting their time returning to the pump every ten to fifteen miles.

Likewise, if you usually tackle just one meal at a time, you have much to gain by rethinking this practice. Your best route out from under the daily food grind is to establish a system that easily, effectively, and indefinitely cuts your time, while also cutting your costs and increasing the nutritive value of your food.

A class notebook was a positive tool for me in school and a Kitchen Notebook provides that same type of lifeline for me now. Just as my class notebooks contained all the relevant facts and information that I needed to pass each course, my Kitchen Notebook contains all the recipes and data that make food management a breeze.

Establishing a Kitchen Notebook takes a little effort and time up front, but when you think about the hours you spend each week eating, not to mention how long it takes to commute to and from the stores/restaurants/delis, to purchase your food, put it away, prepare, serve, and clean up the meals, you begin to understand that there are hours of time savings to be realized.

The Kitchen Notebook itself can be either a traditional student notebook or a special file in your home computer. I began my own notebook many years ago with a 9 by 12-inch, three-ring binder with a 3-inch spine—a basic large notebook. We now have a computer, but it is not near the kitchen and I somehow prefer the handiness and portability of my old and trusty notebook.

As we progress through this chapter, you will be introduced to the value and convenience of creating specialized notebook sections including a Master Shopping List, a Master Price List, a Recipe Roster, and a Daily Food Diary. You should separate these sections with notebook dividers that have pockets, because the pockets will allow you to store loose pages or recipes or clippings until you have a few minutes to incorporate them into the binder itself. If you choose to use a computer to hold your Kitchen Notebook, just create separate file headings for each notebook section.

The Master Shopping List

A logical first step in the timesavings process is to create a Master Shopping List. How many times during the past month have you had to stop by the supermarket for a missing dinner component or other needed items? For a period of time, this was my habit—and it was a major drain on my schedule and food budget.

Gopher trips to the supermarket cost extra in every way—gas, money for impulse items that aren't necessary but look appealing, and time spent driving, standing in line, and unpacking. The simple act of creating a Master Shopping List section within your Kitchen Notebook can help eliminate all this wasted time and effort—and expense—and will enable you to meet all your grocery needs in just one trip per week.

Label your first notebook divider *Master Shopping List.* On a blank sheet of paper, write down everything you buy including food and nonfood items. While grocery stores offer thousands of options, you will find that your list is relatively short (mine contains fewer than two hundred items and that is *everything* I need). The reason the stores maintain such a diversity is because every shopper is different—some prefer this brand or that of whole wheat bread, while others make their own from frozen bread dough, and yet others make bread from scratch with their bread machine.

To help you identify which items you need to include on your list, flip through your recipe cards and books, and peek in your cupboards, refrigerator, and freezer to refresh your memory. Once you have your inventory list, organize the items by category: dairy foods, frozen foods, produce, baking supplies, paper products, and cereals. By grouping similar items, you'll save time in the store by eliminating the need to backtrack through the supermarket aisles.

Make three copies of your categorized list. As you use these during the next few weeks, you will most likely think of a few items that you missed. Add them. When you are confident your list is complete, rewrite or type it in the format you prefer and make several copies. Post one on your kitchen bulletin board. As your week proceeds, highlight items as you use them up. Your grocery list will evolve effortlessly in this manner.

The extra copies should go into your Kitchen Notebook. Again, having one convenient place where you keep track of all your food-related information offers you the control you need to succeed.

The Master Price List

Once your Master Shopping List is complete, the next step is to invest in a pocket-size spiral notebook. Even though this is not a part of your Kitchen Notebook, it is the single most important tool you can use to reduce your food spending, and now is the time to get started. The beauty of creating a separate and portable notebook is that it acts as a miniature data bank, providing you with price comparison information *while you shop.* Never again need you waste money on something you *think* is a bargain, but isn't.

To start your Master Price List, dedicate individual pages of your mini-notebook to each food or nonfood category such as dairy, produce, meats, and so on. Following each heading, such as dairy, enter shopping list items that apply, like eggs, 1% milk, whipping cream, and so on. Leave about ten spaces between each of these subheadings for the next step.

Once you have entered each item from your Master Shopping List, begin recording the standard (nonsale) price for each. Make sure to include the store name, the size of the box or can or bag or whatever, and the price.

The easiest way to fill in this data is to go through your itemized cash register receipts. For items you haven't purchased in a while, you may need to spend a few extra minutes jotting in details while on a special grocery store excursion dedicated to the completion of this project.

Too hard? Hardly! A completed Master Price List offers you the ability to save a lot of money in a short period of time. My Master Price List showed me that I was wasting hundreds of dollars per year. Even better, it provided quick, easy, and painless solutions. For example, I used to buy jars of peanut butter every week. When I began purchasing them only when they went on super-saver sales, about once every six months, I saved. Similarly, frozen whipped topping went on sale for less than one-third of its regular price about once every four months. At those times, I'd stock up. These two changes alone saved our family over $75 that first year. Just imagine the savings *you* will enjoy when you multiply this habit by the two hundred or more items on your list!

If you follow the newspaper ads and weekly sales flyers for your favorite stores, add their comparative sale prices to your Master Price List, again including the relevant information—date, brand, size, and sale price. The ten spaces you left under each item will provide ample space for updates, so that you won't have to replace your personalized-price-prompter for years.

If you shop for food and household items at a warehouse or price club, you know that it's hard to predict what items they'll have—since most clubs don't advertise their products or sale prices. But if you go shopping with your comparison list, you'll know when the club price is a true bargain—and when you can get a better deal elsewhere. My Master Price List entries look something like the entries at right.

By using a Master Price List, you will probably start to see sale patterns: Certain items that go on sale every other week, every six weeks, every six months, and so on. This information helps you plan ahead so you can stock up when the price is lowest. At these times, you can purchase enough to last until the next price-buster sale even if storage space is limited.

To gain maximum savings from your Master Price List, you should coordinate it with your Master Shopping List. If one store is consistently lowest in price on a certain item, write the name of the store to the left of that item on your Master Shopping List. You might also note the date (usually a certain month or week) at which the price is at rock bottom. You can then wait to purchase certain items until you're in the right store—and you can stock up when the price is most friendly. By coordinating your two lists, you can realize huge savings in both time and money.

Buy Food and Household Products in Bulk

My family's food bill dropped dramatically once I started to buy in bulk, and I saved even more time—time I once spent shopping for items I hadn't anticipated needing. My switch to bulk buying, however, required me to think creatively about my storage situation. Our home didn't have a pantry, and those extra rolls of on-sale paper towels, not to mention jumbo-size boxes of powdered milk, rice, and oatmeal required shelving that we didn't have—at first. In search of a solution, I found the advice of Amy Dacyczyn, who in her book *The Tightwad Gazette* (New York: Random House, 1995) says, "If you were offered $50 per month to rent out the space under your bed, would you do it? People tend to think that all food must be stored in kitchen cabinets. However, a closet can be converted to a pantry and unused spaces, such as under your bed, can store a case of bargain

---

American Cheese:

1 ounce = 107 calories/ 8.4 grams fat

Red Owl	5 pounds/$13.87 standard
February	5 pounds/$9.90
Wally's	5 pounds/$14.55 standard
June	5 pounds/$9.80
Wally's	2 pounds/$6.67 standard
March	2 pounds/$3.89

Cheddar Cheese:

1 ounce = 112 calories/ 9.1 grams fat

Food Club	16 ounces shredded/$3.00 standard
December	16 ounces shredded/$2.23
Red Owl	8 ounces shredded/$1.75 standard
May	8 ounces shredded/$.99

Nonfat Cottage Cheese:

1 ounce = 80 calories/ > 1 gram fat

Super Value	24 ounces Land O Lakes/$2.79 standard
January	24 ounces Land O Lakes/$1.89
Super Value	24 ounces Bridgeman/$2.69 standard
May	24 ounces Bridgeman/$1.79

Cream Cheese, Reduced-Fat:

1 ounce = 25 calories/ 0 grams fat

No sales. Available only at Doug's.

Cream Cheese, Regular:

1 ounce = 99 calories/ 9.9 grams fat

Red Owl	8 ounces/$.89 standard
March	8 ounces/$.48
Super Value	8 ounces/$.95 standard
June	8 ounces/$.69

---

canned pineapple. Buying in bulk can save the average family at least $50 per month."

My own solution was to have a set of storage shelves built under the stairwell and to put a spare freezer in my laundry room. Yours may be to turn the hall closet into a pantry. Wherever you put your bargains, you will gain both freedom and control by creating a pantry stocked with foods and household staples that you know you will use.

I stock at least one extra "unit" of each nonperishable item on my Master Shopping List, and store or freeze larger quantities of foods that go on super sales. When I open my replacement or notice my supplies dwindling, I highlight the ingredient on my Master Shopping List. When shopping time arrives, my list is ready. I simply add store names, brands, sizes, and sale prices. There is no time wasted deciding what I need, just whether to buy a single replacement unit or a whole case.

One of the most exciting discoveries I made during my trek toward food freedom was the realization that maintaining a stocked pantry gave me the freedom to make *anything* in my recipe collection *anytime* I wanted to. Gone was the discouragement of having to rule out numerous menu ideas simply because I was missing one or more of the ingredients and didn't have the time, energy, or money to go to the store again.

As you incorporate these strategies into your lifestyle, you will notice a decrease in food spending, an increase in free time, and a definite sense of being prepared. It is a great feeling to know that no matter what meal is ahead, or who may join you at the last minute to share it, you are equipped to make any recipe that comes to mind.

The Recipe Roster

Having food items on hand doesn't do much good unless you can find the recipe you want. If you are like me, you own a whole bunch of cookbooks with about two recipe favorites in each. Spending time searching for just the right recipe is frustrating. The solution? Start a section in your Kitchen Notebook for your own exhaustive Recipe Roster. Begin by writing the names of recipe categories (for example, Desserts, Fix-It-Fast, Pasta Entrées, Soups, Sandwiches, Veggie Side

Dishes) on several pages in your notebook. You might even want to allow a full page for each category so that your Recipe Roster has room to grow.

When you use a favorite recipe, check to make sure it is entered in your roster. If not, take a moment to write in the recipe name, as well as the page number and title of the book from which it came.

Next to each of my recipe entries I write down the calorie count, fat grams, and dollar cost because these are important to me. You may be interested in how long it takes to assemble each recipe or the sodium content. Entering your key statistics as you go allows you to make decisions that are in line with your dietary, financial, or time limitations without the hassle of refiguring each component each time.

If keeping track of those loose recipes written on scraps of paper is a problem, tape them onto full-size sheets of paper and add these to your notebook. Number the pages and enter each recipe name and page number into your roster. I tape quite a few recipes to each page and can always find the one I want.

The Daily Food Diary

If cutting fat is as important to you as cutting time and money, a strategy that works is to write down every bite you eat. Chances are you nibble more often than you think. And having a written record in your Kitchen Notebook may show that your diet is not as balanced as you had thought. Only as you identify a dietary leak can you take the appropriate action to fix it. Included in the Daily Food Diary section of my notebook are personal weight goals, an exercise plan, and my devotional commitments—we need spiritual nourishment at least as much as nutritional.

Personalize Your Kitchen Notebook

Other notebook divisions may feature a freezer inventory, an entertaining record with dates, guest lists, and menus, or a section for additional cooking charts and tips. Insert originals or photocopies and keep making entries in the index.

By all means keep your notebook within easy reach of your cooking center. It will become the first place you look for food-related data. If you cannot find a needed chart or recipe today, take the time to add the information once you do find it. It only takes a few seconds to add it to your Kitchen Notebook, but it could save you precious minutes later.

It is said that successful people are willing to do things that unsuccessful people are not. Creating a Kitchen Notebook requires a bit of time and commitment up front, but it is one of the strategies that virtually guarantees a return of time and money savings down the road.

3.

Cut Your Costs
by Shopping Smart

Entering a grocery store with shopping list in hand is the first sign that you are taking your food spending seriously. Supermarket managers are anxious to relieve you of as much of your income as they can; tempting and appealing silent sales pitches are everywhere throughout grocery stores and it is *your* assets they are targeting.

Unfortunately, resisting the impressive aisle-end displays is only your first step in protecting your discretionary dollars. Much thought has gone into every aspect of grocery store layouts. Eye-level and easy-to-reach places are reserved for goods with the highest markups, while the more cost-effective choices are relegated to top or bottom shelves and are usually put in the center aisles, less obvious to the casual shopper.

Thanks to marketing geniuses, you will need to think of yourself as a strategic planner in a battle of sorts: you and your money on one side and the advertisements and store layouts on the other. Defend your hard-earned money by using the figures in your Master Price List as a guide for determining which sales are really good deals, and shore up your defenses even further by limiting your purchases to items highlighted on your Master Shopping List.

Studies have shown that the average food shopper spends four hours' worth of wages in just seventeen minutes, so your goal should be to minimize the amount of time you spend shopping for food. One way to accomplish this is to keep your pantry stocked with one or more "units" of all the food and household items you use on a regular basis. Another way is to be creative and savvy about substitutions. I rely heavily on the Substitutions and Equivalents guide beginning on page 178, as it contains hundreds of options that allow me to use what I have in my cupboards instead of wasting time and money on additional grocery store encounters. Delaying a front-line skirmish by even a day or two improves the bottom line.

Strategies for Winning the War at the Supermarket

When the inevitable shopping trip arrives, it can only help your cause if you are aware of some of the tactics used in this particular type of warfare. The Standard Directory of Advertisers discloses that, in a one-year period, Pillsbury had advertising expenditures of $473 million; the Kraft General Foods outlay ran just over $500 million. You're up against big bucks and powerful marketing resources, but there are things you can do.

Buy Generics Rather Than Brand Names   Assuming that name brands contain higher-quality ingredients than generics is not necessarily accurate. And don't believe that, just because a brand-name product costs more, it's any better—or better for you—than another brand or a generic. The difference in price can often be attributed to advertising costs, and not to any real difference in ingredients.

Be Careful with Those Coupons   Cents-off coupons are simply another form of advertising. They encourage shoppers, just as do TV commercials, to purchase name-brand products. The informed shopper would subtract the price of the coupon from the cost of the advertised product. Compare that figure to the best deal in your Master Price List and buy the product or toss the coupon according to your findings.

Resist Attractive Packaging   Another marketing strategy involves the actual packaging of processed foods. I get a kick out of the photos on the box covers of frozen dinners. Don't they look appetizing? If you are a regular frozen dinner consumer, you will understand my amusement: What you see is rarely what you get.

Sidney Margolius, in his fascinating expose, *The Great American Food Hoax* (New York: Walker, 1971), explains that ready-to-heat dinners tend to cost more than twice as much as equivalent versions prepared at home. This would not be so bad, although a significant cost over time, if the ingredients were less adulterated with fillers such as starch, sauces, breading, and thickeners. Breading in heat-and-serve chicken dinners accounts for nearly 40 percent of the weight of the small pieces. Frozen egg rolls need to contain only 10 percent meat to meet United States Food Standards; chicken chop suey and chow mein need to contain only 4 percent meat. If you want suggestions on how to prepare meals that are similar in concept but far superior to packaged foods, turn to the chapters entitled Save Time and Money by Cooking in Quantity (page 36) and Cut Your Time by Working Smart in the Kitchen (page 22). You'll find that great taste at a great price doesn't take a lot of hours.

Build a Better Breakfast   A major sinkhole for unsuspecting shoppers is the cold cereal section. Advertisers would have us believe that the most nutritious way to start our day is with these packages of, and I quote, "corn, sugar, salt, corn syrup, malt syrup and annatto extract color." Of course, "BHT is added to packaging material to preserve freshness" as are the vitamins and minerals that were stripped out in the production process.

Many cereals cost more per pound than fine steak, and none less per pound than chicken. Nutritious options such as toast, peanut butter, and juice allow you to sleep just as late and pocket a couple hundred bucks a year, depending on how much you buy now, of course. If you want to start your day with cereal, check out the recipe for granola on page 158. It's nutritious, delicious, and won't break your budget. If you want to make the change in your breakfast habits a tasty adventure, check out *The American Country Inn and Bed and Breakfast Cookbook*, Volumes I and II, by Kitty and Lucian Maynard (Nashville, TN: Rutledge Hill Press, 1990, 1993). They feature more than 1,700 recipes from 500 American inns.

Make Friends with Your Butcher   Most butchers are happy to slice, sliver, or shave packaged meats bought from their department. I buy 95 percent fat-free turkey hams when they go on sale for one-quarter the price of deli ham. If I make the meat department my first stop, the ham is usually cut and packaged before I finish my other shopping.

While prepackaged slicing usually comes free in a meat department, nothing else does. Buying precut chickens is an expensive proposition, while whole, uncut chickens are reasonably priced and yield two breasts, two wings, two legs, and two other pieces. Many recipes call for deboned breast pieces, the most expensive chicken option. I usually cut up two chickens, as shown in the illustration at right, and serve everything but the breasts for one meal, reserving the breasts for the more fancy entrées. The two chickens cost about the same amount as a package of three breast pieces alone, so I gain a single breast plus twelve other pieces by doing my own cutting.

The only kind of precut chicken I buy is chicken legs, as these go on sale for about half the price of even the least expensive whole, uncut chickens.

When it comes to ground meat, I purchase the lower-in-fat ground turkey. If you have ever tried a pound of turkey burger and were turned off, there was probably just cause. Some of the brands I have tried were nearly tasteless and full of gristle. The only brand I can recommend without reservation is Shenandoah. This brand is usually available in the freezer section in one-pound tubes. It is regularly 50¢ less a pound than regular hamburger, and sometimes goes on sale for 40 percent off that price. If your grocer does not stock this brand, send a note of encouragement with this address: Shenandoah, 100 Quality Street, Bridgewater, VA 22812.

While spending less on groceries is a rewarding activity, there are times when spending more can be just as rewarding. Take advantage of as many saving tips as work for you and then enjoy your extravagances without guilt. You have earned them!

Make the Price Club and Food Co-op Connection

Warehouse clubs that offer food products provide bulk goods at often remarkable savings. Most clubs sell produce, meat, and dairy products as well as grocery staples and items such as paper plates, cups, and zip-top bags (not to mention lawn mowers and office supplies).

CHICKEN CUTLERY FOR SAVINGS

1. Begin by removing any loose pieces from the inside of the bird. Rinse the chicken and then cut the wing portion from the body, rotating the wing as needed to help the separation.

2. Bend the leg joint back and cut through the meat and skin until the hip joint is free. Cut *around* the bone, not through it.

3. Cut toward the drumstick to separate it from the thigh.

4. Hold the body (neck end down) and remove the backbone by cutting down along each side of the bone and through the rib joints.

5. Cut a V through the white cartilage at the neck, exposing the dark bone at the center of the breast.

6. Remove the bone by bending the breasts back and forth. Cut the two breast meat pieces apart with a knife.

Cutting Up a Chicken

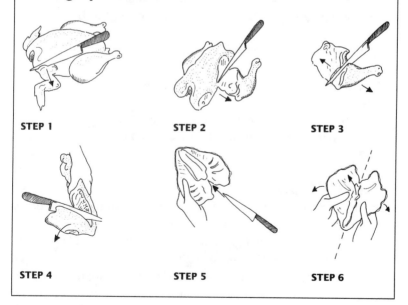

STEP 1   STEP 2   STEP 3

STEP 4   STEP 5   STEP 6

They can be excellent sources for inexpensive breakfast foods including oatmeal, dried fruits, and peanut butter.

Warehouse clubs such as Price-Costco and Sam's are usually located in or near large cities and require annual membership fees. In return, shoppers have access to savings of up to 35 percent on bulk purchases.

Club veterans advise the use of a master price list, a calculator (unit prices are usually not posted and some warehouse prices are higher than your best buys elsewhere), and a lot of common sense. Limit purchases to items you are sure you will use before they spoil. If you end up throwing away the food, it wasn't a good deal.

To find out if there is a club near you, check your Yellow Pages under Department Stores. I know it's odd to look for groceries in a department store, but there it is. You might prefer to call one of the numbers listed below to find out if these national chains have a store near you.

BJ's (57 stores nationwide)
1-800-257-2582
(Open Monday to Friday, 9 A.M. to 5 P.M.)

Price-Costco (200-plus stores in the U.S.A.;
50-plus stores in Canada, Mexico, and England)
1-800-774-2678
(Open Monday to Friday, 8 A.M. to 5 P.M.)

Walmart's Sam's Club (2,080 stores nationwide)
1-701-795-9449
(Open Monday to Friday, 10 A.M. to 8:30 P.M.,
Saturday, 9:30 A.M. to 8:30 P.M., and Sunday,
12 noon to 7:00 P.M.

Food co-ops are quite different from warehouse clubs. First, whereas warehouse clubs are about the size of two gigantic grocery stores, co-ops are usually small to the point of being claustrophobic. The majority of co-ops do not charge membership fees and do not require minimum purchases, but some do.

Food co-ops offer savings to a broader base of shoppers because they can be found in even the smallest communities and have no membership limitations. I buy all my spices through a food co-op because the savings are pretty impressive (see the following chart).

Unlike warehouse clubs, most co-ops allow customers to purchase any quantity they desire. An easy first step into buying co-op spices is to purchase just the amount your empty spice container can hold (most are between .4 and 2 ounces). If you decide to take advantage of the tips in the chapter entitled Dry Mix Magic (page 59), larger quantities will come in handy.

In the city where I live, we have a small group called the Warroad Food Club. We order from a catalog of options one month and the following month a semitruck delivers the composite order to a location decided upon by the group. The members who help unload and divide up the goods receive a discount on their bill, while those who come just in time to collect their groceries pay full price (still significantly less than regular).

In the closest big city, Grand Forks, North Dakota, there is a food co-op that operates a small storefront. One person serves as manager and earns a salary, while other members work for discounts on their groceries. You can shop there whether or not you are a member, and the prices on most things are significantly less than their grocery

COMPARISON OF SUPERMARKET VS. FOOD CO-OP PRICES ON VARIOUS SPICES

Ingredient Name	Size	Supermarket Price	Size	Co-op Price	Savings per Pound
Allspice, ground	.75 oz.	$2.09	1 pound	$2.65	$41.93
Chili Powder	4 oz.	$4.39	1 pound	$2.78	$14.78
Cinnamon, ground	1 oz.	$1.77	1 pound	$3.25	$25.07
Onion Flakes	3 oz.	$3.29	1 pound	$3.30	$14.24
Pepper, black	4 oz.	$2.85	1 pound	$3.95	$7.45

store counterparts. The major savings are realized on spices, staples, cheese, nuts, and dried fruits.

If the community where you reside is heavily populated, there is most likely an existing food co-op of some type. Check the Yellow Pages under Grocers, Health Foods, and Natural Foods. If you are unable to locate a co-op locally, contact the Department of Agriculture, the State Department of Consumer Affairs, a television news desk, or the food editors at your local newspaper. If no club is available, you may be interested in searching out ten or more families with similar values who would like to help you start your own.

To learn more about food co-ops (sometimes called clubs), consider contacting a warehouse that services your area. Here are a few suggestions:

Blooming Prairie Natural Foods
510 Kasota Avenue Southeast
Minneapolis, MN 55414
800-322-8324 in Minnesota
800-328-8241 outside Minnesota
Supplier for Minnesota, eastern North Dakota, South Dakota, northern Wisconsin.

Blooming Prairie Warehouse, Inc.
2340 Heinz Road
Iowa City, IA 52240
319-337-6448
Supplier for Illinois, Iowa, northern Kansas, Michigan, Missouri, Nebraska, southern South Dakota, southern Wisconsin, southwestern Wyoming.

Federation of Ohio River Cooperatives
320 Outerbelt, Suite E
Columbus, OH 43213
614-861-2446
Supplier for northern Georgia, southeast Indiana, Kentucky, Maryland, northern North Carolina, Ohio, western Pennsylvania, Tennessee, Virginia, Washington, D.C., West Virginia.

Hudson Valley Federation
6 Noxon Road
Poughkeepsie, NY 12603
914-473-5400
Supplier for Connecticut, northern New Jersey, New York, eastern Pennsylvania.

Mountain People's Warehouse
12745 Earhart Avenue
Auburn, CA 95602
916-889-9531
Supplier for Arizona, California, Colorado, Idaho, Montana, Nevada, New Mexico, Oregon, Utah, Washington, Wyoming. Special arrangements available for Alaska and Hawaii.

NutraSource
4005 Sixth Avenue South
Seattle, WA 98108
800-33-NUTRA   Washington: 800-762-0211
Supplier for Washington, Idaho, Oregon, Alaska.

Ozark Cooperative Warehouse
PO Box 1528
Fayetteville, AR 72702
501-521-4920
Supplier for Alabama, Arkansas, Florida, Georgia, Kansas, Louisiana, Mississippi, Oklahoma, Tennessee, Texas.

Tucson Cooperative Warehouse
350 South Toole
Tucson, AZ 85701
800-350-2667   Arizona: 602-884-9951
Supplier for Arizona, Southern California, Colorado, Las Vegas, Nevada, New Mexico, West Texas, Utah.

4.

Cut Your Time by Working Smart in the Kitchen

Taking charge of your supermarket visits gives you a financial edge; likewise, taking charge of your kitchen gives you an edge on time, and can free up the extra hours most cooks crave.

Organize Your Kitchen for Speed

Imagine working in an office where your desk is across the room from the telephone and computer. Now look around your kitchen. Are there things you can change or rearrange to make it a more efficient work space?

Bonnie Runyan McCullough, author of *Bonnie's Household Organizer* (New York: St. Martin's Press, 1980), is my favorite home management consultant. Her book has helped thousands of home managers gain extra hours in their days. The chapter dealing with kitchen management encourages the use of four work centers: a mixing center, a cooking center, the sink, and the table.

Once you have determined where each of these areas will be in your kitchen, designate prime shelf space in each area to the supplies needed there, and relegate those less frequently used to cupboards that are farther away. Think through how you use your utensils and cooking supplies, place them in drawers or cupboards close to the area in which they will be most often used. Coffee cups might go above the coffeemaker. Measuring spoons, cups, and mixing bowls will go near where you assemble mixes. Alphabetize your spices and put them away in the correct order after each use. A few simple changes can save you many hours over the course of a year.

Clean Up as You Go

Keeping your sink filled with hot, soapy water while you cook allows you to wash dishes as you go instead of letting the mess pile up. If this is not your style, consider using a "dishwasher with sponge," available at most grocery stores or from Arrow Plastic Mfg. Co., Elk Grove Village, IL 60007. Ask for #007. These handy little sponges attached to the end of a soap-filled handle work especially well for washing out measuring cups, glasses, and deep mixing bowls.

Make Utensils Serve Double Duty

The most useful measuring cups I have are glass with handles. These allow me to measure and microwave in the same dish and they are available in two-, four-, six-, and eight-cup sizes. Measuring scoops are also convenient in that they allow you to eliminate the step of scooping the flour into the measuring cup.

Flour sifters can be replaced with a fork or wire whisk. Just fluff up the flour before scooping out the amount required and again after combining the dry ingredients.

A versatile tool that is underused in most kitchens is the blender. It will crush crackers, make bread crumbs, chop vegetables, and stir up ingredients for sauces, salad dressings, and beverages. Cleaning the unit is simple if you fill the emptied blender container half full of warm water and add a squirt of dish soap. Cover and whir on high for about a minute, then rinse and invert.

Master Your Microwave

For quick cooking, thawing, and reheating plus myriad other time-consuming jobs, nothing compares with the microwave. Because this unit cooks foods so quickly, it is imperative that you know if your machine is the standard 600 to 700 watts. If not, use the following chart to adjust time requirements as needed:

TIMING ADJUSTMENT CHART FOR MICROWAVES		
600- to 700-watt ovens use cooking times given in recipes:	500- to 600-watt ovens add 15% to cooking time:	400- to 500-watt add 35% to cooking time:
15 seconds	17 seconds	20 seconds
30 seconds	35 seconds	40 seconds
1 minute	1 minute 10 seconds	1 minute 20 seconds
2 minutes	2 minutes 20 seconds	2 minutes 40 seconds
3 minutes	3 minutes 30 seconds	4 minutes
4 minutes	4 minutes 35 seconds	5 minutes 25 seconds
5 minutes	5 minutes 45 seconds	6 minutes 45 seconds
10 minutes	11 minutes 30 seconds	13 minutes 30 seconds
15 minutes	17 minutes 15 seconds	20 minutes 15 seconds
20 minutes	23 minutes	27 minutes
25 minutes	28 minutes 45 seconds	33 minutes 45 seconds
30 minutes	34 minutes 30 seconds	40 minutes 30 seconds

A conventional oven recipe can be microwaved if you start checking for doneness after approximately a quarter of the suggested cooking time. For example, if a recipe calls for sixty minutes in the oven (regardless of temperature), start checking after fifteen minutes in the microwave. Continue cooking, checking often and rotating your dish a quarter turn each time you check, until it is done. Make a note of how long it actually takes for future reference.

Besides reducing baking times, the microwave offers numerous shortcuts to otherwise boring or messy tasks.

- Spare yourself a dirty pan by sautéing onions in the microwave. Place ½ cup diced onions and 1 tablespoon margarine in a microwave-safe dish; cover and cook on high for 2 to 3 minutes, stirring after each minute.

- Cook corn on the cob by placing unhusked ears on a paper towel in the microwave. Cook on high for 3 to 4 minutes per ear (or 10 to 11 minutes for four ears). Remove with pot holders and slide off husks and silk.

- Scald milk in a glass measure on high. It takes just over 2 minutes per cup of milk.

- Melt marshmallow cream on high for 30 to 45 seconds per 7-ounce jar.

- Defrost 8 ounces of whipped topping on medium for 1 minute.

- Crisp stale pretzels, snack chips, or crackers on high for 30 seconds; let stand 1 minute before serving.

- Soften rolls by wrapping each in a napkin or paper towel and microwaving on medium low for 15 to 30 seconds. Serve immediately.

- Maintain a moistureproof environment to melt chocolate chips or squares without caking. Cook on high for 1 minute, stir vigorously, and microwave at additional 30-second intervals, stirring well between each, until smooth.

- Soften butter or cream cheese on high for 15 seconds per 4 ounces.

- Toast coconut until golden by cooking on high for 1 to 2 minutes.

- Roast nuts on high for 3 to 4 minutes, stirring after each 60-second interval.

- Soften lumpy brown sugar by microwaving it with a slice of bread in a covered dish on high for 30 to 60 seconds.

- Dry fresh herbs between layers of paper toweling by microwaving on high for 2 to 3 minutes. Let rest for 3 minutes and test to see if they are dry to the touch. If not, microwave at additional 30-second increments until dry.

- Crisp 4 slices of bacon between paper towels on high for 3 minutes.

- Defrost a loaf of frozen bread dough by placing it inside a plastic bag and microwaving it on high for 1 minute. Let stand for 2 minutes, rotate, and microwave for an additional 30 seconds. Portions of the dough will toughen if overcooked. Let the dough rest at room temperature for a few minutes, check again, and microwave at additional 10- to 15-second intervals until thawed.

Your family no doubt has certain recipes that everyone enjoys week in and week out, month after month. Start a special Tried-and-True section in your Kitchen Notebook for these recipes, and add to it (one recipe per page) when you develop or find new ones. The nine recipes that follow are the old standbys in our family, and you may find they work in your home, too. These have given me the ability to wait until the last minute before even thinking about dinner. If you like the idea of having numerous choices at your fingertips, you could find many more options by checking out the *Better Homes and Gardens Fix It Fast Cook Book* (Des Moines, IA: Meredith Corp., 1979). Each recipe requires four or fewer ingredients and goes together quickly. Another book that has been useful to me is *Six Ingredients or Less: Cooking Light and Healthy*, by Carlean Johnson (Gig Harbor, WA: CJ Books, 1992).

Nine Timesaving, Quick-and-Easy, Tried-and-True Recipes

Turkey Salsa Quickies

Use deli turkey or leftovers for this 3-minute meal.

Ingredients	Quantity
Turkey meat, cooked and diced	1 cup
Salsa (page 119)	2 cups
Sour cream	1 cup
Tortillas	8
Shredded Cheddar cheese	¼ cup
Yield	4 servings

Combine the meat, salsa, and sour cream. Layer some of the mixture in the center of each tortilla, then roll (log-style) and place, seam side down, in a glass baking dish. Cover with plastic wrap and microwave on high for 3 minutes, sprinkle with Cheddar cheese, and microwave uncovered for an additional 30 seconds, until cheese is melted.

Optional: Garnish with sour cream and diced onion, tomato, and lettuce.

Yorkshire Strata

Served with a pretty fruit salad, the soufflé frame and Worcestershire gravy turn otherwise boring leftovers into a very impressive dinner.

Ingredients	Quantity
Cooked meat	1 cup
Cooked, diced vegetables	½ cup
Water	½ cup
Beef or chicken gravy (see Gravy Mix, page 81)	1½ cups
Worcestershire sauce	1 tablespoon
Onion powder	1 teaspoon
Margarine	2 tablespoons
Milk	1 cup
Eggs	2
Flour	1 cup
Salt	¼ teaspoon
Pepper	⅛ teaspoon
Yield	6 to 8 servings

Combine meat, vegetables, water, ¼ cup of the gravy, Worcestershire, and onion powder; set aside. Place margarine in a 10-inch pie plate and set in cold oven. Turn heat to 425°F.

In a blender container, combine milk, eggs, flour, salt, and pepper; blend on high for 45 seconds. Remove the hot pie plate and pour in the batter. Spoon meat mixture into center, leaving at least 1 inch around the edges. Return pie to oven for 30 minutes (do not open oven door). Remove directly to table where guests are waiting. Serve with heated gravy.

Chicken in a Jiffy

If you have chicken thawed and company on the way, try this quick, delicious solution.

Ingredients	Quantity
Margarine	4 tablespoons
Chicken pieces	3 to 4 pounds
Spike or seasoning salt	1 tablespoon
Sliced mushrooms	2 cups fresh or 4 ounces canned
Yield	4 to 6 servings

Melt margarine in bottom of a 9 by 13-inch pan. Roll chicken in margarine to coat; sprinkle generously with spike. Bake with meaty side up in 450°F oven for 25 minutes. Remove pan from oven long enough to pour over the mushrooms, including liquid if canned. Return all to oven for 5 minutes. Serve with gravy made from chicken drippings (see Gravy Mix on page 81).

Turkey Rice Pilaf

Ingredients	Quantity	2X Quantity
Chicken soup base (see *Bouillon*, page 183)	2 tablespoons	3 tablespoons
Water	2 cups	4 cups
Uncooked long-grain white rice	1 cup	2 cups
Frozen peas	1¼ cups	2½ cups
Turkey meat, cooked and cubed	2 cups	3 cups
Cream of chicken soup (page 73)	1¼ cups	2½ cups
Slivered almonds	½ cup	½ cup
Yield	4 to 6 servings	10 to 12 servings

Bring soup base and water to a boil; add rice, reduce heat, cover, and simmer for 20 minutes. Cook peas according to package instructions; add the turkey and soup; heat until warmed through. When the rice is cooked, fold all together with almonds, reserving a few for garnish.

Turkey Meatballs Tetrazzini

Ingredients	Quantity	2X Quantity
Ramen noodles and seasoning pack, separated	1 3-ounce package	2 3-ounce packages
Meatballs	8	16
Cream of chicken soup (page 73)	1¼ cups	2½ cups
Parmesan cheese	¼ cup	¼ cup
Yield	4 servings	8 servings

Cook noodles as directed while browning frozen or freshly made meatballs. Combine soup and seasoning pack; mix well. Fold together cooked meatballs, drained noodles, and soup combination; garnish with Parmesan cheese.

Fridge Biscuit Entrées

Inexpensive refrigerator biscuits offer speedy dinner options that kids and grown-ups enjoy.

Press individual biscuits into 10 greased muffin tins, making a well in the center of each. Fill the wells with one of the following:

- A combination of browned ground meat and BBQ sauce topped with a few sprinkles of Cheddar cheese.

- A combination of condensed cream of chicken soup or gravy plus leftover turkey or chicken meat plus leftover peas or carrots, topped with a few sprinkles of Cheddar cheese.

- A combination of diced ham and blender-puréed cottage cheese, topped with Cheddar cheese.

Freeze until firm, then remove to an airtight container for later use, or bake at 425°F for 10 minutes and serve hot.

Another great option is to roll out biscuits with a rolling pin and let kids make their own mini-pizzas with ingredients of their choice. Freeze or bake at 425°F for 8 to 10 minutes.

Incredible Edible Venison Steaks

If you're like me and have a hard time with the wild taste of venison but have a freezer full of the stuff, you will enjoy this unusually easy and truly delicious recipe.

Slice venison steaks into ¼-inch-thick fillets. Pound both sides with a meat mallet until steaks are about ⅛ inch thick. Heat an ungreased electric skillet to 375°F. Dust each fillet with unseasoned flour (I shake fillets in a zip-top bag with about ½ cup flour); shake off excess and set aside.

Slide 1 tablespoon margarine around the bottom of skillet to coat, then quickly add a single layer of fillets. Fry for 2 minutes (until slightly browned), then turn and fry until sizzly and a bit golden; do not overcook.

Remove to serving plate and sprinkle generously with salt and pepper. Cover fillets while you finish remaining steaks. Serve hot.

Caution: Adding seasonings before frying will toughen steaks.

Poppin' Pizza

When the gang votes for pizza but both the pocketbook and cook dread the thought, use this magic dough recipe and save big bucks over takeout and major minutes over traditional recipes.

Crust ingredients	Quantity	2X Quantity
Milk	½ cup	1 cup
Oil	1 teaspoon	1 tablespoon
Flour	½ cup	1 cup
Eggs	1	2
Yield	2 to 4 servings	4 to 6 servings

Combine all ingredients in blender container and whir on high until smooth (about 45 seconds). Set aside.

Place the following ingredients in a greased 8 by 8-inch pan (9 by 13 inches for larger quantity).

Pizza sauce (see Pizza Seasoning Mix, page 86)	10 ounces	20 ounces
Pizza meat	½ cup	1 cup
Grated cheese	3 ounces	6 ounces
Other favorite ingredients as desired		

Pour the crust combination over all and bake at 400°F for 30 minutes. Serve immediately.

Meatballs Consommé

Rich flavor without the fat and without the cost of a tin can.

Ingredients	Quantity
Ground beef	1 pound
Egg, beaten	1
Bread crumbs or oatmeal	½ cup
Dry onion flakes	1 tablespoon
Cold water	2 cups
Beef soup base or bouillon (see *Bouillon*, page 183)	2 teaspoons
Tomato paste	½ teaspoon
Cornstarch	2 tablespoons
Yield	4 to 6 servings

Combine ground beef, egg, bread crumbs, and onions; form into 1-inch meatballs. Brown and set aside. Mix remaining ingredients and pour into skillet. Heat, stirring constantly, until thickened. Add meatballs and simmer, covered, until heated through. Serve hot or keep warm in 350°F oven for up to 1 hour.

Serving suggestion: We prefer this over mashed potatoes, but it works fine with rice or egg noodles, too.

---

* Specific consommé instructions on page 115.

5.

Save Time and Money by Cooking in Quantity

At one time or another you may have had enough casserole left to freeze for reheating later, or maybe you have even doubled a recipe with the express goal of freezing the extra for a future meal. This kind of "expansion cooking" makes good sense. If you are going to mess up the kitchen and spend your precious moments preparing a made-from-scratch dish, why not make it count?

Even if you have limited pans, mixing bowls, and utensils, you can make your own convenient frozen dinners at a fraction of what you would pay for highly processed ones from the supermarket. The following list of hints and tips should convince you that cooking in quantity can truly expand your time and budget.

THE HOWS AND WHYS OF COOKING IN QUANTIT.Y

HERE'S HOW	HERE'S WHY
■ For huge batches, make use of electric skillets, Dutch ovens, and Crock-Pots.	■ You can make a lot more food in the same amount of time by taking advantage of these additional cooking appliances.
■ Keep your freezer at 0°F.	■ This is a safe temperature for all frozen foods.

HERE'S HOW

- Slightly undercook noodles, rice, and potatoes that are to be frozen and reheated later.

- If using a tomato sauce, do not precook the pasta. Be sure the noodles are completely covered with sauce. This works well for spaghetti, lasagne, manicotti, etc.

- Ground meat can be browned, drained, and frozen on cookie sheets until firm, then transferred to freezer-quality bags and returned to the freezer.

- When freezing layered dishes like lasagne, place a large enough piece of heavy-duty aluminum foil in your baking dish to allow you to fold it over the top. Assemble the ingredients as directed, seal tightly, and freeze in pan. When frozen, pop out the foil package, label and date it, and return the entrée to the freezer until needed. To use, slip off the tinfoil jacket under warm running water and place the frozen entrée in the original baking dish. Cook as directed.

HERE'S WHY

- They have a tendency to dry out if overcooked.

- The sauce will separate slightly in freezing and the noodles will cook in the water while baking. Excess water is absorbed, yielding a thick, rich sauce.

- This allows meat to be measured out in exact amounts as needed and requires less time to thaw.

- This technique allows you to prepare numerous entrées ahead of time without investing in additional baking dishes. Also, the foil packages take up much less space in the freezer than do pans and casserole dishes.

THE HOWS AND WHYS OF COOKING IN QUANTITY

HERE'S HOW

- Use freezer-quality zip-top bags when possible. Layered dishes require above treatment, but most other foods freeze well in zip-tops.

- Reuse freezer-quality bags until they get a hole; then discard.

- Do not freeze foods in wax paper, regular aluminum foil, or regular zip-top bags.

- Label packages well. Include entrée name, date assembled, and cooking instructions.

- Use masking tape to seal packages.

- When you are making two or more batches of an entrée, do similar tasks all at once. For example, place the first layer of noodles in all the pans, then the first layer of sauce in all pans, etc.

HERE'S WHY

- These bags hold more food than seems possible. They also freeze flat and take up much less room in your freezer.

- These bags are expensive but durable. A single hole in a bag can ruin an entire dinner, however, so always run water into the bag while washing and check to make sure no holes exist.

- These substances are not durable enough for freezing purposes.

- Meals have a tendency to look alike once frozen. Including use instructions saves you looking it up later.

- Costs less than freezer tape and works better than transparent tapes.

- This saves time and mental energy because it requires that you read the recipe only once and you do each preparation task only once.

THE HOWS AND WHYS OF COOKING IN QUANTITY

HERE'S HOW	HERE'S WHY
■ Refreeze meat or prepared foods only if you have altered their consistency by cooking. In other words, do not thaw a pound of hamburger, make meatballs, and return the meatballs to the freezer unless you have cooked the meat. If you want to make a big batch of meatballs without cooking them, prepare the meatballs while the ground beef is still fresh.	■ Reduces risk of freezer burn and rancidity.
■ Unless you are very familiar with your microwave's defrost functions, avoid defrosting frozen entrées in the microwave.	■ Most microwaves start cooking portions of the entrée before the entire entrée is even thawed.

More Secrets for Successful Cooking in Quantity

Casserole Magic   The most obvious recipes to expand are casserole dishes that include noodles and rice. Assemble the extra meals while you are making tonight's dinner, but freeze them before baking. When you cook them immediately prior to use, the aroma and fresh taste will make you think the dish was just assembled. The recipe for Layered Tamale Pie (page 45) is one of our favorite expandable casserole entrées. Since this is a layered dish, I use the tip about lining extra baking dishes or bowls of similar size with heavy-duty aluminum foil for the extra meals. To expedite assembly, I place the bottom tortilla in each dish, then a layer of sauce in each, and continue in assembly-line fashion as directed.

One note about freezing Cheddar cheese: If it comes in contact with aluminum foil it can actually eat a hole in the foil. To avoid this, wait to add the shredded cheese until just before you bake the dish.

Two more layered dishes that are easy to prepare, freeze well, and taste great when thawed and cooked are Spaghetti Pie (page 46) and Layered Turkey Bake (page 47).

If a recipe you wish to increase does not provide instructions for reheating from frozen, use this basic rule: Remove the dish from its freezer wrapping and place it, still frozen, in a covered casserole dish in a cold oven. Turn the oven to 350°F and bake for approximately half again the originally recommended cooking time (for example, if the recipe calls for 30 minutes baking time, bake it for 45 minutes), uncovering the dish halfway through. Test for doneness by feeling a knife that has been inserted into the center of the casserole. If the knife comes out hot, the dish is done. If not, recover the casserole and keep cooking. Unless otherwise noted, most casserole dishes keep nicely in the freezer for up to six months.

Freezing Meats, Poultry, and Fish   There is no need to limit your expanding activities to casseroles; fried or broiled meat and poultry pieces are also excellent freezer options. Divide the portions you wish to save into serving-size, freezer-quality containers; label and freeze for up to six months. Thaw in the refrigerator and serve cold, or unwrap while still frozen and place in a 350°F oven until heated through. The time will vary significantly with the thickness of your meat, so check it frequently.

Cooked sliced meats are another freezable option if they are covered completely with a sauce or gravy. Thaw in the refrigerator and reheat in a covered baking dish at 350°F for about 1 hour.

For whole, sliced, or slivered ham and turkey ham, simply divide into serving-size quantities, place in zip-top bags, and freeze for up to 3 months without added sauces or gravy. Thaw in the refrigerator overnight, drain excess liquid, and prepare as desired. One of my favorite lunches to serve guests, Creamy Ham Croissants (page 48), takes advantage of cubed turkey ham that I purchase on sale and keep in my freezer. The recipe calls for croissants, which you can make yourself (see page 153), or they can be purchased frozen from the freezer section at your grocery store. Your warehouse club bakery department may provide a fresh, price-conscious solution. You will have to purchase a box, but if you have a freezer, these freeze well and are always a fancy addition to brunch or lunch.

My family and I live just one mile from Lake of the Woods on the Canadian border and we take advantage of the fishing. When the fish are biting, we usually bring home more than we can eat all at once, and if I am going to do a fish fry, including the mess of hot oil, I make the most of it. I fry up every last fillet (see Incredible Fried Fish on page 49) and then freeze the leftovers in freezer-quality zip-top bags for excellent fishwiches—fish fillets served in hamburger buns with Miracle Whip or Tartar Sauce (page 50).

Freezer Solutions for Pizza, Soups, Stews, Stuffings, Snacks, Desserts

Homemade pizzas are always in demand. Assemble extra pizzas, wrap well, label, and freeze until needed. To cook, place the unwrapped frozen pizza on a baking sheet and bake at 425°F for 15 to 20 minutes. Uncooked pizzas will keep in the freezer for up to 1 month, although a lock on your freezer door may be the only way to accomplish that feat! One of my favorite ways to make pizzas for the freezer is with the recipe for Pizza Roll-Ups on page 52.

Soups and stews freeze well if you avoid potatoes and slightly undercook the vegetables and noodles. If you wish to freeze a cream soup, omit the thickeners until you reheat the combination. To serve, heat from frozen in a heavy saucepan over low heat. As it thaws, break apart the main chunk with a fork. Add thickeners and any additional seasonings as required, heat through, and serve.

Stuffing is a great side dish and keeps well in the freezer for up to 1 month. If left in a cooked turkey, stuffing can be unsafe, so remove all of the stuffing before proceeding with your other dinner responsibilities. Any leftover stuffing should be cooled to room temperature, placed in freezer-quality containers, labeled, and frozen. Later, unwrap and bake in a covered casserole dish at 350°F for 20 minutes. Remove the cover and continue baking for 10 minutes longer. If you enjoy the convenience of boxed stuffing mixes, you can save a small fortune and turn out superior stuffing every time with the recipe for Seasoned Stuffing Mix on page 54.

Expand your horizons even farther by creating exciting fruit side dishes in quantity. I keep a large supply of Frosty Fruit Cups (page 55) in the freezer and call on them often to round out a variety of meals. Fancy and festive, they work well for breakfast, brunch, or dinner.

Be sure to include desserts in your expanding repertoire. Frozen desserts keep for months and offer great comfort when unexpected guests arrive on your doorstep. One of the crowd pleasers at our house is Frozen Mud Pie (page 56).

Snacks and treats also freeze well. You can make your own slice-and-bake cookie dough using your plastic-wrap box to create a mold for the dough. Tear off a large piece of wrap and then remove the tube from the box. Use the wrap you just tore off to line the empty plastic-wrap box and spoon in the cookie dough, creating a tube of dough. Seal and label each roll. Store in the refrigerator for up to 3 weeks, or in the freezer for up to 6 months. My hands-down favorite is Slice-and-Bake Chocolate Chip Cookie Dough (page 57).

If you enjoy frozen snacks on a stick, make your own fruit pops for extra nutrition and variety. One of our favorite family recipes is for Frozen Fruit Pops (page 58).

Freezer Dos and Don'ts

While most foods freeze well and are suitable for expanding, the chart on the next page gives the exceptions and the reasons why you should avoid freezing these particular ingredients. For certain foods—such as cream cheese and cottage cheese—I give the caution because the food *sometimes* separates when thawed. In dishes such as lasagne, separation is hard to detect, but for something like cheesecake, separated cream cheese would ruin your presentation.

FREEZER HINTS

DO NOT FREEZE . . .	BECAUSE . . .
■ Cooked egg whites or hard-cooked eggs	■ They become rubbery.
■ Salad dressing or mayonnaise	■ It separates.
■ Milk sauces	■ They may curdle.
■ Carbonated beverages	■ They may explode as they expand. Even if they don't explode, they may be flat when thawed.
■ Meringue	■ It may shrink and ooze.
■ Cream or cottage cheese	■ It may separate or break down.
■ Hard cheese (I freeze any cheese that will be crumbled or shredded for use on pizzas, casseroles, etc. Hard cheese may be frozen in blocks or already shredded.)	■ It crumbles when cut.
■ Yogurt or sour cream	■ It separates.
■ Fresh salad ingredients	■ They wilt when thawed.
■ Gelatins or gelatin desserts	■ They get runny.
■ Creams or custards	■ They become watery and lumpy and may separate.

If you are taking advantage of bulk purchasing and expansion cooking, the possibility of power failure carries with it the threat of wiping out a lot of food and effort. Here are some tips that should provide a little peace of mind should an outage occur, including the reasons why each is valuable.

FREEZER ADVICE FOR A POWER OUTAGE

INSTRUCTION	REASON
■ Keep your freezer door shut.	■ A fully packed freezer will keep food frozen for up to 48 hours if the door is never opened.
■ Order sliced dry ice and place it in the freezer. Use cardboard to keep the ice from coming into contact with the food.	■ This will keep food frozen.
■ Refreeze foods that are still firm or have ice crystals on them.	■ These foods have not suffered damage.
■ Cook and serve, or cook, repackage, and refreeze foods that are cool or partially thawed.	■ These foods would probably get freezer burn if refrozen in their original form.

Layered Tamale Pie

Ingredients	Quantity	4X Quantity
Ground beef	1 pound (1½ cups cooked)	4 pounds
Black olives	4 ounces	1 pound
Tomato sauce	15 ounces	60 ounces
Taco seasoning mix (page 85)	1 package (1½ tablespoons dry mix)	4 packages
Corn tortillas (small)	6	24
Cheddar cheese, shredded	¼ cup	1 cup
Water	⅓ cup	1⅓ cups
Yield	4 servings	16 servings

Combine meat, diced olives, tomato sauce, and seasonings. Place one corn tortilla in bottom of a 10-inch round casserole. Layer on sauce, another tortilla, sauce, tortilla, etc., ending with sauce. Sprinkle with Cheddar cheese and then pour the water around edges of casserole. Freeze or bake, covered, at 400°F for 40 minutes (or at 350°F for 1 hour). Let stand before cutting.

From frozen: Place covered, frozen entrée in cold oven. Turn heat to 375°F and bake for 60 minutes.

.ghetti Pie

Ingredients	Quantity	2X Quantity
Angel hair pasta, cooked	6 ounces	10 ounces
Margarine	1 tablespoon	1 tablespoon
Parmesan cheese	¼ cup	⅓ cup
Eggs, beaten	2	3
Cottage cheese	¾ cup	1½ cups
Ground beef, browned and drained	½ pound	1 pound
Spaghetti sauce seasoning mix (page 87)	1 package (2 teaspoons)	2 packages
Tomato paste	6 ounces	12 ounces
Water	1 cup	1½ cups
Yield	4–6 servings	8–10 servings

Combine drained pasta, margarine, cheese, and eggs. Mix well and form a shell in a 9-inch round pan (9 by 13-inch pan for larger batch). Set aside. In blender container, whir cottage cheese on high until smooth. Spoon it onto the noodle crust. Combine ground beef, seasonings, tomato paste, and water; mix well. Spoon over cottage cheese. Freeze, or bake at 350°F for 35 minutes. Garnish with Parmesan or Cheddar cheese, if desired.

From frozen: Place frozen pie in cold oven. Turn oven to 350°F and bake for 60 minutes.

Note: Noodles must be precooked for this recipe since the sauce does not cover them completely.

Layered Turkey Bake

Ingredients	Quantity	2X Quantity
Seasoned stuffing mix (page 54)	2 cups	4 cups
Margarine	2 tablespoons	4 tablespoons
Water	½ cup	1 cup
Eggs, beaten	1	2
Chicken/turkey meat, cooked and diced	2 cups	3 cups
Cream of chicken soup (page 73)	1¼ cups	2½ cups
Milk	1 cup	2 cups
Yield	4 servings	8 servings

Combine stuffing, margarine, and water. Layer half of mixture in bottom of an 8 by 8-inch pan (9 by 13-inch for larger batch). Mix together eggs and meat and spoon this on top of base layer. Cover with second half of stuffing mixture. Combine soup and milk and stir well. Pour over all and freeze, or cover and bake at 350°F for 35 to 45 minutes.

From frozen: Place covered frozen entrée in cold oven. Heat to 350°F and bake for 50 to 60 minutes.

Creamy Ham Croissants

Ingredients	Quantity	2½X Quantity
Margarine*	2 tablespoons	5 tablespoons
Flour*	2 tablespoons	⅓ cup
Dry mustard	2 teaspoons	1 tablespoon
Milk*	¾ cup	2½ cups
Ham cubes	1 cup	3 cups
Parsley flakes	1 tablespoon	1 tablespoon
Croissants (page 153)	4	10
Yield	4 sandwiches	10 sandwiches

Combine margarine, flour, and mustard over medium-high heat, stirring constantly, until thick and bubbly. Gradually add the milk until blended and then add the ham. Continue stirring until thick and smooth. Remove from heat and stir in parsley. Spoon onto opened croissants and serve warm.

* Substitute an equal quantity of nonfat White Sauce (page 82).

Incredible Fried Fish

Ingredients	Quantity
Flour	1½ cups
Salt	1 teaspoon
Lukewarm water	1½ cups
Oil	6 tablespoons
Fish fillets	2 to 4 pounds
Flour	to coat fillets
Egg whites	2
Yield	6 to 16 servings

Sift together the flour and salt. In a separate bowl combine water and oil. Gently blend in flour combination and let stand at room temperature for 2 hours or longer.* Dredge fillets in flour,** shaking off excess. Heat oil in deep fat fryer to 425°F. Beat egg whites just until they hold their shape: do not overbeat. Gently fold egg whites into room temperature batter. Dip each floured fillet into batter and then into hot oil. Fry until golden on both sides, turning if needed.*** Remove to paper toweling and sprinkle with salt.

freeze in ziptop bags
use as fishwiches w/
Tarter sauce pp 50

* 2 hours is the ideal time for the batter to rest because a fermentation process offers a softer coating. Waiting 20 minutes to 4 hours will yield satisfactory results.

** Use plain flour because seasoning the fillets at this point toughens them.

*** Fry as many fillets at a time as you wish, using a metal spatula to keep them submerged. The batter does not stick or crumble so you can fry many, many fillets at once. Serve with Tartar Sauce (page 50).

Tartar Sauce

Ingredients	Quantity for original version	Quantity for fat-free version
Miracle Whip	2 cups	
Miracle Whip Free		2 cups
Onion, finely diced	1 small	1 small
Dill pickles, finely diced	2 small	2 small
Yield	2 cups	2 cups

Combine all ingredients and serve immediately, or store in an airtight container in refrigerator for up to 6 months.

Shrimp Cocktail Sauce

When the opportunity to have shrimp arrives, you won't want to be without this excellent sauce.

Ingredients	Quantity
Catsup	½ cup
Pickle relish	3 tablespoons
Prepared mustard	1 teaspoon
Worcestershire sauce	dash
Tabasco	dash
Sugar	1 teaspoon
Yield	⅔ cup

Combine all ingredients and mix well. Serve immediately or store in an airtight container in refrigerator or freezer for up to 6 months.

Pizza Roll-Ups

This is my meal of choice when we have to eat in the car. I assemble the roll-up early in the afternoon and pop it in the oven as we are packing.

Thaw a loaf of frozen bread dough according to instructions, but do not allow it to rise. Sprinkle a bit of flour on the counter and roll the dough out to an 8 by 12-inch rectangle.

Leaving a ½-inch space around the edges, layer on 6 ounces Pizza Sauce (page 86) and then the pizza toppings of your choice. Roll it up, log-style, and seal the edges and ends by pinching them together.

Slide the roll onto a greased baking sheet, seam side down. Curve it into a crescent shape and make a few slashes in the top of the dough with a knife. Bake at 325°F for 25 minutes. Let stand for 5 minutes, then cut into slices. Serve on paper plates.

Make as many roll-ups as you want. Freeze the extras for up to 1 month.

Croutons

Here's a recipe that *starts* in the freezer, then is made in quantity for storage at room temperature. My grandmother taught me to save any leftover bread crusts in a bag in the freezer. Then, when I wanted to make croutons for stuffing mix or to top off the perfect salad, I could make them in a flash and at no expense.

Ingredients	Quantity for cheese croutons	Quantity for regular croutons	Quantity for nonfat croutons
Bread cubes	4 cups	4 cups	4 cups
Margarine, melted	6 tablespoons	1½ tablespoons	—
Parmesan cheese	4 tablespoons	—	—
Oregano	½ teaspoon	—	—
Basil	½ teaspoon	—	—
Garlic salt	¼ teaspoon	—	¼ teaspoon
Garlic powder	—	⅛ teaspoon	—
Celery salt	⅛ teaspoon	—	—
Yield	1 cup	1 cup	1 cup

Combine all ingredients and stir to coat. Spread in a baking dish and microwave on high for 3 to 5 minutes, until sizzling and browned, stirring after each minute. Croutons can also be baked at 300°F for 30 minutes, stirring after each 10 minutes. Cool completely and store in zip-top bags at room temperature for up to 6 months.

Seasoned Stuffing Mix

The original recipe equals one 6-ounce box of stuffing mix (approximately 3 cups cooked stuffing.)

Ingredients	Quantity	4X Quantity
Small bread cubes	3 cups	12 cups
Chicken or beef soup base (see *Bouillon*, page 184)	1 tablespoon	3 tablespoons
Onion flakes	2 teaspoons	3 tablespoons
Celery flakes	2 teaspoons	3 tablespoons
Parsley flakes	1 teaspoon	1 tablespoon
Thyme	½ teaspoon	2 teaspoons
Pepper	⅛ teaspoon	⅛ teaspoon
Salt	⅛ teaspoon	¼ teaspoon
Yield (bread crumbs)	3 cups	12 cups
Yield (dry mix seasonings)	5 teaspoons	6 tablespoons

Microwave bread cubes on medium high for 2 to 3 minutes, stirring after each 60-second interval, until dry. Cool completely. Store in a large zip-top bag at room temperature until needed. Combine seasonings separately and store in a small zip-top bag taped to bread cubes bag.

Use instructions:

Dry bread cubes	3 cups
Dry mix seasonings	5 teaspoons
Water	½ cup
Margarine	1 tablespoon
Yield (stuffing)	3 cups

Combine ingredients in a microwave-safe dish and heat on high for 2 minutes. Stir, cover, and let rest for 3 to 5 minutes; fluff up with a fork and serve.

Frosty Fruit Cups

Ingredients	Quantity	2X Quantity
Frozen pink lemonade concentrate	6 ounces	12 ounces
Frozen strawberries, thawed	10 ounces	20 ounces
Fruit cocktail, including juice	15 ounces	29 ounces
Sugar	¼ cup	½ cup
Water	1¼ cups	2½ cups
Bananas, sliced	2	4
Yield (5-ounce dixie cups)	12	24

Combine lemonade, strawberries, fruit cocktail, sugar, and water; stir well. Add sliced bananas and use a soup ladle to fill 5-ounce plastic cups three-quarters full. Freeze. Use cookie sheets to stack the cups in layers in the freezer.

Use instructions: Run hot water over bottoms of cups to loosen fruit; tip into individual dessert dishes, and let stand at room temperature for 15 to 25 minutes. If needed sooner, use a fork to break up the ice. Just before serving, fluff the partially thawed fruit with a fork.

Serving suggestion: Pour a little clear or strawberry-flavored carbonated soda over top of each fruit cup.

Frozen Mud Pie

Ingredients	Quantity	2X Quantity
Chocolate cream-filled cookies	16	32
Instant coffee granules	1 teaspoon	2 teaspoons
Margarine	3 tablespoons	5 tablespoons
Ice cream	2 flavors	2 flavors
Walnuts or pecans	1 cup	2 cups
Toppings, including chocolate and caramel	1 cup	2 cups
Whipped topping	8 ounces	8 ounces
Yield	6 to 8 servings	10 to 16 servings

Crush cookies and coffee granules; combine with margarine and press into an ungreased 9-inch round pan (9 by 13-inch pan for larger batch). Bake in 350°F oven for 8 minutes. Remove and let cool. Press one layer of your favorite ice cream, about ½ inch thick, onto crust. Top with a generous sprinkling of nuts, then a steady, thin drizzle of both toppings. Layer on a different kind of ice cream and repeat nuts and toppings. Continue layers until ice cream is within 1 inch of pan rim. Finish with a generous layer of whipped topping, sprinkling on nuts and making a final decorative drizzle pattern with the toppings. Freeze and then cover with freezer-quality plastic wrap.

To serve: Allow dessert to soften at room temperature for 5 to 10 minutes. Cut and serve.

Substitution options: For a low-fat version, use Nonfat Frozen Yogurt (page 174) and ice cream toppings (Chocolate Syrup, page 147; Caramel Sauce, page 146). If you don't usually purchase Oreo cookies, bake half a batch of Brownies (page 173) in your pan and use that as the crust.

Slice-and-Bake Chocolate Chip Cookie Dough

Ingredients	Quantity
Margarine	¾ pound
Brown sugar	1½ cups
Sugar	1 cup
Vanilla	1 tablespoon
Eggs	2
Flour	3½ cups
Baking soda	2 teaspoons
Salt	1 teaspoon
Yield	6 dozen cookies

Melt margarine in microwave on high for 1 minute. Add sugars, vanilla, and eggs; mix on low with electric mixer until smooth. Combine dry ingredients and add, mixing well by hand. Stir in your choice of optional additions from below and drop by heaping teaspoons onto greased baking sheets. Bake at 325°F for 8 to 12 minutes; cool on racks.

Optional Additions:

Chocolate chips or M&M's: 2 cups
Mini-morsels: 1 cup
Butterscotch chips: 2 cups
Chopped walnuts or pecans: 1 cup

Freezing instructions: Freeze in tube shapes until needed. Slice as many cookies as desired onto greased baking sheets. Bake at 325°F for 10 to 14 minutes. Cool on racks.

Frozen Fruit Pops

Ingredients	Quantity
Orange juice concentrate	½ cup
Milk	⅔ cup
Banana	1
Sugar	1 tablespoon
Yield	8 popsicles

Combine ingredients in blender container and whir on high until smooth. Pour into 8 popsicle molds and freeze until firm (about 3 hours).

Dry Mix Magic

Of the vast collection of modern convenience foods, my favorites are dry package mixes. The simplicity of ripping open an envelope compared to the mess of chopping and measuring is obvious, and food manufacturers use this fact to their advantage. Did you know that the Ranch Dressing Mix recipe on page 77 costs less than a tenth of the supermarket price when you make it at home? If you buy Shake & Bake, you might be surprised to learn that you can coat the same thirty-two pieces of chicken for less than 10 percent of what you would pay in the store with the recipe on page 88. The key to saving money *and* time is to measure out big batches of your favorites. Unlike prepackaged mixes, home versions contain only a few ingredients (all of the unpronounceable ones are unnecessary).

Start Your Own Collection of Homemade Dry Mixes

There is an easy way to develop a pantry full of homemade convenience foods at a fraction of the cost of the store-bought equivalents. Throughout this chapter you'll find numerous dry mix recipes, many of which you will recognize as favorites. Any time you are going to make a meal using a dry mix, take advantage of your time in the kitchen and the fact that you already have all the ingredients out on the counter. Measure the quantity for tonight's dinner into one bowl, and the big-batch quantity into another. Once your dinner is assembled and cooking, take a moment to write a label including the name of the mix, the date you assembled it, and how it is to be used. You will soon have a cupboard full of dry mix options that will save you a fortune—and the time investment is almost nil.

If creating a dry mix collection all at once suits you, start by flagging the recipes you want to assemble. Make sure you have the required ingredients on hand and arrange them and all needed measuring utensils and storage containers on your counter. Assemble one mix after another until your dry mix collection is complete—all in one session.

Use moistureproof, airtight, containers with good seals or tight-fitting lids. Practically any clean container with a tight-fitting lid would offer suitable storage; some of my favorites include sour cream and cottage cheese containers. For large batches, I use clean, dry, ice cream buckets, deli containers, or even empty oatmeal containers. For small batches, freezer-quality zip-top bags work great. An empty shoe box or other similar-sized container works well as a "file cabinet" for dry mixes in zip-tops. Of course, you should never use a container that has previously contained a harmful substance, even if you wash it out.

Label your mixes as you prepare them. They will look alike later, so do it immediately. I prefer self-adhesive labels, available from office supply stores, but writing on masking tape works, and even a square of paper with the name of the mix, date assembled, and use instructions written on it can be taped to your container for quick identification. However you decide to do it, be sure to do it as you go.

For no-fuss cooking, I place additional labels on the exterior of large batch containers, including instructions for the recipes I use most often that involve that mix. Later I just grab the container and cook from those instructions instead of hauling out a cookbook. Once I have a storage container labeled, I use it over and over for the same mix, thus eliminating relabeling. Since these are *dry* mixes, I just wipe the inside with a damp cloth, dry it out, and let it sit until the next assembly session.

Mass quantity dry mix assembly will go more quickly if you use two sets of measuring utensils: one for dry ingredients and the other for shortening. I keep a few paper towels handy to wipe out opposing flavors like pepper and sugar, but I do not clean between flavors that more or less blend.

When measuring shortening (which happens repeatedly during a major assembly session), try this trick. If you need 2 cups of shortening, pour 2 cups cold water into a 4-cup glass measure. Spoon the shortening into the water, pressing down as needed to keep it submerged, until the water/shortening combination increases the volume to 4 cups. Hold a few fingers over the shortening, invert the cup over the sink, drain the water, and you are left with exactly 2 cups of shortening without the sticking or air pockets that so frustrate an otherwise smooth assembly process. If you need only ½ cup shortening, pour 2 cups cold water into the measuring cup, add shortening until the total comes to the 2½-cup level, pour off the water, and there is your ½ cup.

If you want to make a big batch of a dry mix recipe, but you have never tried it and are not sure you will like it, simply make your "trial" recipe and leave out all the dry ingredients until after you have taste-tested the final product. If it passes the test, quickly measure out your big batch, label it, and save time and money from now on! If not, put the ingredients away and you have wasted no time or ingredients.

This final assembly tip can be a lifesaver if interruptions are as common in your home as they are in mine. When a recipe requires, let us say, 8 cups of flour, place 8 tokens (coins, pens, whatever is handy) in front of the flour canister. As you measure, move the tokens, one for each cup, to the other side of the mixing bowl. Even if the phone rings or your toddler spills his milk, you will know exactly how much flour you still need to add.

The time savings available with dry mixes is exciting! If you have some traditional recipes that you make repeatedly, consider rewriting them to take advantage of this. I rewrote my chili recipe (which we loved but I didn't make too often because it required time-consuming chopping and dicing). Now I can throw it together in seconds. If anyone noticed a difference, they never said so. I'll show you how I did it farther on. Before you consider rewriting one of your own favorites, be sure to check the "Dry Mix" heading in the index to see if I have already done the work for you. If your favorite is not listed, bombs away!

The first step is to decide if your recipe would be more cost effective and/or less time consuming in dry mix format. Take advantage of the Substitutions and Equivalents Guide (page 178) to identify how many of the fresh or liquid ingredients in the recipe could be changed to a dry, room-temperature substitute. This is how my favorite brownie recipe appeared in its original form:

Marnie's Favorite Brownie Mix (Before)

¾ cup sugar

1 cup flour

½ teaspoon salt

4 eggs, slightly beaten

10 tablespoons butter, melted

12 ounces chocolate chips, melted

2 teaspoons vanilla

Mix and spread all ingredients in greased 9 by 13-inch pan. Bake at 350°F for 30 minutes.

The only dry ingredients listed in the original recipe are sugar, flour, and salt, but the Substitutions and Equivalents Guide (page 178) shows that the butter can be replaced with butter-flavored shortening, which has a shelf life of six months. The chocolate chips can be replaced with unsweetened cocoa and extra sugar and butter-flavored shortening. The only remaining ingredients are eggs and vanilla. Here is the revised recipe with a few other changes that I will explain in a moment:

Marnie's Favorite Brownie Mix (After)

Ingredients	Quantity	4X Quantity
Flour	1 cup	4 cups
Sugar	2 cups	8 cups
Unsweetened cocoa	¾ cup	3 cups (8 ounces)
Salt	½ teaspoon	2 teaspoons
Shortening (butter-flavored is best)	1 cup	4 cups
Yield (dry mix)	4½ cups	18 cups

Combine dry ingredients; cut in shortening. Store in moistureproof, airtight containers at room temperature for up to 6 months.

Use instructions:	Small	Original
Eggs	2	4
Vanilla	1 teaspoon	1 teaspoon
Dry mix	2¼ cups	4½ cups
Chopped nuts/coconut (optional)	½ cup	1 cup
Yield	12 brownies	24 brownies

Combine eggs and vanilla, beat until foamy. Add dry mix and stir until well blended. Pour into an 8 by 8-inch greased pan (9 by 13-inch pan for larger batch). Bake at 350°F for 25 minutes. Cool and serve plain or frosted.

Useful Hints for Making Your Own Dry Mixes

You may have noticed that the ingredient lists in all my recipes are arranged in reverse order: ingredient on the left, quantity on the right. This allows you to see at a glance which ingredients to assemble, and then to write in your own expanded or reduced quantities at will.

When I rewrite recipes, I often personalize them by changing quantities to make them more useful for me. For the "After" version of the Brownie Mix, I expanded the dry mix portion so I could make a big batch. As you adapt your recipes to meet your needs, each becomes more valuable. Write notes directly on them—they are not fine art. They are your tools, and writing on them makes them more useful.

If the recipe you are converting uses shortening, remember to include instructions to cut it in *after* the dry ingredients have been combined. Also, the shelf life should be noted as six months *minus* the number of months the shortening can was opened before the mix was assembled. For example, if you opened your shortening can in June and assembled your mix in September, you should make a note on the dry mix label indicating that it will expire in December. Dry mixes assembled at home without shortening do not usually require expiration dates.

As noted, unsweetened cocoa powder is a possible substitute for baking chips or chocolates. However, if your end product relies on the bonding agent in the chocolate chips or squares to help hold its shape, as in mousse or candy recipes, cocoa powder will not work.

Not all recipes are as conducive to dry mix revision as the brownies were. Crème de Menthe Syrup, for example, is one of my favorite toppings and adds a touch of class to so many desserts. Since I can make my own in three minutes from scratch for just a sixth the cost of the store-bought version, I won't save much time by having it available as a dry mix. And since the majority of ingredients are not available in dry form, transferring it to a dry mix just wouldn't work anyway. Here's the liquid mix recipe, in case you want to make it in quantity.

Crème de Menthe Syrup Mix

Ingredients	Quantity	_X Quantity
Water	⅔ cup	
Light corn syrup	⅓ cup	
Peppermint extract	¾ teaspoon	
Green food coloring	6 drops	
Yield	1 cup	

Stir all ingredients to combine. Store indefinitely in an airtight container at room temperature.

If the recipe you are considering contains a majority of liquid ingredients even after you have exhausted every possible substitution, it is best to leave it in its original form.

Another favorite recipe, Sopaipillas, is ruled out as a dry mix because of its numerous steps. While I highly recommend these as impressive appetizers for a Mexican meal, the recipe is simply too complicated to be successfully converted to a dry mix. Here is the regular recipe.

Sopaipillas

Ingredients	Quantity	_X Quantity
Milk	1½ cups	
Yeast	1 tablespoon	
Flour	4 cups	
Baking powder	1 teaspoon	
Salt	1 teaspoon	
Butter	1 tablespoon	
Oil for frying		
Yield	70 sopaipillas	

Scald milk; let cool. Activate yeast in ½ cup warm water. Combine flour, baking powder, and salt; cut in butter. Add 1 cup of the cooled milk and the yeast mixture. Toss gently and add just enough of the remaining milk so dough holds together. Knead on lightly floured surface fifteen times. Proceed, or cover and freeze or refrigerate until needed. When ready to use, let (thawed dough) stand at room temperature for 10 minutes. Heat 4 inches of oil to 375°F. Divide dough in half and roll first half to ¼-inch thickness. Cut dough into 2- to 3-inch squares and drop each into hot oil, forcing under until puffed. Allow to brown on one side, flip, and hold under until golden. Remove to paper towels and serve hot with honey.

Marnie's Favorite Chili (Before)

At first glance, my chili recipe appeared to have too many fresh and liquid ingredients to convert to a dry mix.

1 pound ground beef

¼ cup diced onion

1 small garlic clove

1½ tablespoons flour

½ teaspoon chili powder

¼ teaspoon ground cumin

½ teaspoon salt

Drop of Tabasco sauce

15 ounces tomato sauce

½ cup water

1 15-ounce can undrained kidney beans

Brown the ground beef, onion, and garlic; drain fat. Stir in remaining ingredients except beans. Simmer, covered, for 30 to 40 minutes, stirring occasionally, until flavors blend. Add the beans and cook until heated through.

Here is the same recipe after substitutions were made:

Marnie's Favorite Chili Seasoning Mix (After)

Ingredients	Quantity	10X Quantity
Flour	1½ tablespoons	1⅛ cups
Onion flakes	1 tablespoon	¾ cup
Chili powder	½ teaspoon	3 tablespoons
Salt	½ teaspoon	2 tablespoons
Ground cumin	¼ teaspoon	1 tablespoon
Sugar	¼ teaspoon	1 tablespoon
Cayenne	Sprinkle	2 teaspoons
Garlic powder	Sprinkle	½ teaspoon
Yield (dry mix)	3 tablespoons	30 tablespoons

Combine all ingredients and store indefinitely in a moistureproof, airtight container at room temperature.

Use instructions:

Dry mix	3 tablespoons
Ground beef, browned	1 pound
Tomato sauce	15 ounces
Water	½ cup
Kidney beans, including liquid	15 ounces
Yield (6 to 8 servings)	Equivalent to 2 25-ounce cans chili with beans

Combine all ingredients in a saucepan, bring to boil. Reduce heat and simmer for at least 20 minutes, covered. Stir often.

In this example, the chopping of onions and peeling of garlic cloves has been eliminated by conversion and the Tabasco sauce was converted to cayenne. All of the ingredients were then placed in order, with the dry ones listed first and the "last-minute" ones listed under them. With these simple revisions, the goodness of homemade chili is captured in an inexpensive, quickly assembled recipe.

When looking for ingredients to convert, remember that anything requiring refrigeration needs to be replaced by a room-temperature alternative. A few examples include substituting powdered milk for liquid, dry mustard for regular, or butter-flavored shortening for margarine. Some substitutions, such as onion powder for onions, cayenne for Tabasco sauce, and sugar for honey may surprise you. Checking the Substitutions and Equivalents Guide (page 178) thoroughly ensures that you will not miss any timesaving options.

Take care when dealing with seeds or flakes such as onion flakes, red pepper flakes, celery seeds, etc. When you use these flakes, it will take your recipe at least 20 minutes of simmering or 4 hours of refrigeration (for recipes like salad dressings or dips) to blend satisfactorily. If speed is paramount, opt for powders (such as onion powder, cayenne, celery salt, etc.) over flakes. Chili powder is the only powder that requires extra time: Simmer foods including this spice for at least 15 minutes for best results.

Most dry mix recipes can be increased or decreased without adverse affect. If you use large quantities of corn bread, for example, you may wish to assemble a big batch of dry mix. Do this by multiplying the base quantity of each ingredient by whatever number of mixes you are interested in making and then proceed as directed. It takes no longer to measure out ½ cup baking powder than it does to measure out 2 teaspoons, but by doing it all at once you will save time later. You can do something else during the time it would have taken to take out all the ingredients and measure each one again (and again the next time, and the next time, and so on).

Corn Bread Mix

Ingredients	Quantity	2X Quantity	8X Quantity
Flour	1 cup	2 cups	8 cups
Cornmeal	½ cup	1 cup	4 cups
Sugar	¼ cup	½ cup	2 cups
Baking powder	2 teaspoons	4 teaspoons	3 tablespoons
Salt	½ teaspoon	1 teaspoon	2 teaspoons
Yield (dry mix)	1½ cups	3 cups	12 cups

Combine all ingredients and store indefinitely in a moistureproof, airtight container at room temperature.

Use instructions:

Dry mix	1½ cups
Egg	1
Milk	1 cup
Oil	¼ cup
Yield	12 muffins or 1 8 by 8-inch pan

Mix all ingredients until just blended. Pour into greased muffin tins, corn bread tins, or an 8 by 8-inch pan. Bake at 425°F as follows: muffin or corn bread tins for 18 minutes; 8 by 8-inch pan for 20 to 24 minutes. Serve warm or freeze until needed.

You will notice that the yield of dry mix has been translated into the single batch amount under Use instructions. If you are rewriting a recipe, you will want to measure the quantity of your combined ingredients carefully and enter that figure on your recipe under Yield. It is important actually to measure and not simply add up the total of all the individual ingredients to arrive at this number: Powdered spices may "hide" between flaked onions, parsley, etc., and your figure may be off enough to ruin a dish.

To determine how much you would need for each batch, divide the total yield by the number of times you multiplied the recipe. For example, if you multiplied the ingredients by 5, you will want to divide the total yield by 5 to determine the quantity required under Use instructions. Shake your mix well before you measure and also be sure to shake it up again immediately before you measure out the quantity needed for any given recipe.

To help me quickly increase or decrease amounts of any given ingredient, I created a chart that I refer to as my Up-and-Down Chart (see page 72). The figures are approximate, but I have used them for my own rewriting adventures for many years and feel confident that they are close enough for this purpose. The Original column equals the amount called for in your original recipe. If you wish to make half a batch, use the figures under ".5"; if you wish to make a triple batch, use the figures under "3x," etc.

A few other favorite charts appear in Appendix I, but I like to keep The Up-and-Down Chart with my dry mix assembly information for checking as I go. If super convenience interests you, make a photocopy of this chart and tape it inside one of your kitchen cupboard doors.

Finally, a word of caution regarding increasing spice quantities: Some spices, such as chili powder, pepper, and dry mustard, could ruin your mix if you multiply them up to the same degree as milder spices such as nutmeg, paprika, and onion powder. The recipes in this book show that multiplying up is safe in *most* instances. You will soon get a feel for how much spice you prefer in your mixes, but, until then, double the amount of questionable or strong spices called for in the original recipe only every third or fourth increase.

THE UP-AND-DOWN CHART

				Approximate Figures						
.25X	**.33X**	**.5X**	**Original**	**2X**	**3X**	**4X**	**6X**	**8X**	**10X**	**12X**
Sprinkle	Sprinkle	Sprinkle	⅛ tsp	¼ tsp	⅜ tsp	½ tsp	¾ tsp	1 tsp	1¼ tsp	1½ tsp
Sprinkle	Sprinkle	⅛ tsp	¼ tsp	½ tsp	¾ tsp	1 tsp	1½ tsp	2 tsp	2½ tsp	1 tbls
Sprinkle	⅛ tsp	¼ tsp	½ tsp	1 tsp	1½ tsp	2 tsp	1 tbls	4 tsp	5 tsp	2 tbls
⅛ tsp	¼ tsp	½ tsp	1 tsp	2 tsp	1 tbls	4 tsp	2 tbls	8 tsp	10 tsp	4 tbls
¼ tsp	½ tsp	1 tsp	2 tsp	4 tsp	2 tbls	8 tsp	4 tbls	5 tbls	7 tbls	8 tbls
½ tsp	¾ tsp	1½ tsp	1 tbls	2 tbls	3 tbls	¼ cup	⅓ cup	½ cup	⅔ cup	¾ cup
1 tsp	2 tsp	1 tbls	2 tbls	¼ cup	⅓ cup	½ cup	¾ cup	1 cup	1¼ cups	1½ cups
1½ tsp	1 tbls	2 tbls	¼ cup	½ cup	¾ cup	1 cup	1½ cups	2 cups	2½ cups	3 cups
2 tsp	4 tsp	2½ tbls	⅓ cup	⅔ cup	1 cup	1½ cups	2 cups	2⅔ cups	3⅓ cups	4 cups
1 tbls	2 tbls	¼ cup	½ cup	1 cup	1½ cups	2 cups	3 cups	4 cups	5 cups	6 cups

Marnie's Cream of "Anything" Soup Mix

These dry mixes replace the store-bought canned versions that are so versatile in the kitchen. There are no cans to recycle and no additives or preservatives. Also, while a can of cream of chicken soup tallies up 330 calories, 23.8 fat grams, and 2,370 grams of sodium, this home version weighs in at only 95 calories, .2 fat grams, and 710 grams of sodium, and at roughly a tenth the cost. You save in every way!

Ingredients	Quantity	9X Quantity
Nonfat dry milk powder	¼ cup	2 cups
Cornstarch	4 teaspoons	¾ cup
Chicken soup base (see *Bouillon*, page 183)	1½ teaspoons	5 tablespoons
Onion flakes	1 teaspoon	2 tablespoons
Thyme	Dash	1 teaspoon
Dill weed	Dash	1 teaspoon
Celery salt	Dash	1 teaspoon
Yield (dry mix)	⅓ cup	Equivalent to 9 11-ounce cans

Mix all ingredients and store indefinitely in a moistureproof, airtight container at room temperature.

Use instructions:

1 can cream of chicken soup = ⅓ cup dry mix plus 1¼ cups water

1 can cream of mushroom soup = ⅓ cup dry mix plus 1¼ cups water plus 2 ounces finely chopped mushroom pieces plus 1 teaspoon salt

1 can cream of celery soup = ⅓ cup dry mix plus 1¼ cups water plus ⅛ cup celery flakes or ½ cup chopped celery, microwave in water until soft

   To serve: Combine ingredients and heat until thickened, stirring constantly.

   For use in casseroles: There is no need to combine the dry mix with liquid before adding it to the other casserole ingredients. Simply mix the dry mix with the dry casserole ingredients, then mix the liquid with the casserole's other liquid ingredients. Cook as directed.

"Cream of Anything" Vegetarian Soup Mix

Ingredients	Quantity	6X Quantity
Vegetable soup base (see *Bouillon*, page 183)	3 tablespoons	1¼ cups
Onion flakes	2 tablespoons	¾ cup
Cornstarch	1 tablespoon	⅓ cup
Parsley flakes	2 teaspoons	¼ cup
Yield (dry mix)	¼ cup	1½ cups

Combine all ingredients and store indefinitely in a moistureproof, air-tight container at room temperature.

Use instructions:

Dry mix	¼ cup
Milk	2 cups
Water	1 cup
Puréed cooked vegetables (choose from asparagus, carrots, cauliflower, celery, broccoli, onion, peas, potatoes, spinach, corn, or mushrooms)	1½ cups
Yield (soup)	3 cups

Blend the dry mix into the milk and water and microwave on high until heated through, about 4½ minutes. Add the puréed vegetables and heat until warm. Add salt and pepper as desired and serve hot.

Note: Purée the cooked vegetables of your choice in the blender on high for about 45 seconds. If you are blending very hot veggies, be sure to start the blender on low with the center cover removed: Hot liquids expand and may explode if closed in and turned on high.

Broth Mix

Recipes for broth from stewed chickens and other ingredients abound, and grocery stores offer 10-ounce cans for under a dollar. This recipe provides ecology (no cans to discard), economy, no additives, no preservatives, no colorings, and terrific convenience.

Ingredients	Quantity	8X Quantity
Chicken or beef soup base (see *Bouillon*, page 183)	3 tablespoons	3 cups
Cornstarch	2 teaspoons	⅓ cup
Parsley flakes	1 teaspoon	3 tablespoons
Yield (dry mix)	⅓ cup	3½ cups

Combine all ingredients and store indefinitely in a moistureproof, airtight container at room temperature.

Use instructions:

Dry mix	2 tablespoons
Cold water	1¼ cups
Margarine	1 teaspoon
Yield	10 ounces

Combine all ingredients and microwave on high until boiling (about 2 minutes). Stir vigorously and use as directed in recipe.

Creamy Italian Dressing Mix

So easy and so good!

Ingredients	Quantity	4X Quantity
Nonfat dry milk powder	2 tablespoons	½ cup
Italian seasoning	1 teaspoon	1 tablespoon
Garlic powder	½ teaspoon	2 teaspoons
Onion powder	½ teaspoon	2 teaspoons
Yield (dry mix)	2 tablespoons	½ cup

Combine all ingredients and store indefinitely in a moistureproof, airtight container at room temperature.

Use instructions:	Quantity for regular version	Quantity for fat-free version
Dry mix	2 tablespoons	2 tablespoons
Mayonnaise	1 cup	
Fat-free mayonnaise		1 cup
Water	6 tablespoons	½ cup
Yield (dressing)	1¼ cups	1⅓ cups

Blend all ingredients well and refrigerate for several hours before serving. Keep refrigerated.

Ranch Dressing Mix

This is a terrific mix to have on hand for homemade salad dressings and hors d'oeuvres. The homemade version costs about 15¢ per recipe. How much have you been paying?

Ingredients	Quantity	_X Quantity
Nonfat dry milk powder	¼ cup	
Garlic powder	1 teaspoon	
Onion powder	1 teaspoon	
Sugar	1 teaspoon	
Dill weed	½ teaspoon	
Salt	½ teaspoon	
Dry mustard	⅛ teaspoon	
Yield (dry mix)	⅓ cup	

Mix all ingredients and store indefinitely in a moistureproof, airtight container at room temperature.

Use instructions:	Quantity for regular version	Quantity for nonfat version
Dry mix	⅓ cup	2 tablespoons
Mayonnaise	1 cup	
Fat-free mayonnaise		⅓ cup
Water	¼ cup	
Lemon juice	4 teaspoons	
Liquid nonfat milk		1 cup
Yield (dressing)	1 cup	1 cup

Combine all ingredients and mix well. Refrigerate for a minimum of 3 hours to blend flavors.

Coleslaw Spice Mix

This spicy mix will add excitement to your coleslaws—at less than *1 percent* of the cost of store-bought brands.

Ingredients	Quantity	4X Quantity
Sugar	⅓ cup	1 ⅓ cups
Salt	¼ teaspoon	1 teaspoon
Celery salt	¼ teaspoon	1 teaspoon
Onion powder	⅛ teaspoon	¼ teaspoon
Dry mustard	⅛ teaspoon	⅛ teaspoon
Pepper	Sprinkle	Sprinkle
Yield (dry mix)	⅓ cup	1 ⅓ cups

Combine all ingredients and store indefinitely in a moistureproof, airtight container at room temperature.

Use instructions:

Dry mix	1 tablespoon plus 2 teaspoons
Water	2 tablespoons
Mayonnaise*	⅜ cup
Shredded cabbage	4 cups
Yield (coleslaw)	4 cups

Combine the dry mix, water, and mayonnaise; blend. Pour the combination over the cabbage and stir well. Chill for at least 4 hours before serving.

* You can replace mayonnaise with fat-free mayonnaise for a nonfat product.

Biscuit Mix

Use the original version any time a recipe calls for Bisquick, pancake mix, or muffin mix. The defatted version tastes much like the boxed variety at an incredible savings of 70 grams of fat per recipe. The whole wheat recipe can be substituted cup for cup in recipes calling for biscuit mix.

Ingredients	Quantity for original version	6X quantity	Quantity for defatted version	Quantity for whole wheat version
All-purpose flour	1⅞ cups	11 cups	1⅞ cups	2 cups
Whole wheat flour	—	—	—	3 cups
Baking powder	4 teaspoons	½ cup	4 teaspoons	2 tablespoons
Salt	½ teaspoon	1 tablespoon	½ teaspoon	2 teaspoons
Shortening	⅓ cup	2 cups	—	1½ cups
Sugar	—	—	2 tablespoons	—
Nonfat dry milk powder	—	—	3 tablespoons	—
Yield (biscuit mix)	2 cups	12 cups	2 cups	6 cups

2 cups data: Original @ 1,378 calories/72 grams fat; defatted @ 820 calories/2 grams fat; whole wheat @ 1,606 calories/58 grams fat

Instructions for Original or Whole Wheat Mixes

Combine dry ingredients, cut in shortening. Store for up to 6 months in an airtight, moistureproof container at room temperature.

Instructions for Defatted Mix

Combine ingredients and store in an airtight, moistureproof container at room temperature until needed. Mix requires the addition of ⅓ cup liquid nonfat milk per 2 cups dry biscuit mix. Since liquid nonfat milk cannot be stored at room temperature, add it immediately prior to use and keep any unused batter refrigerated. Make a note on your recipe or on the container of dry mix that whenever you use this mix, ⅓ cup liquid nonfat milk should be added to the recipe. Further defat your life by replacing milk and eggs with liquid nonfat milk and egg substitutes in any recipe.

Recipe options:

Dropped Biscuits

Stir together 2 cups mix and 1 cup milk until just moistened. Bake at 400°F on a greased cookie sheet for 8 to 10 minutes.

Rolled Biscuits

Stir together 2½ cups mix and ⅔ cup milk. Knead ten times, then roll out to ½-inch thickness and cut as desired. Bake on a greased cookie sheet at 450°F for 8 to 10 minutes.

Pancakes

Stir together 2 cups mix, 1 cup milk, and 2 eggs until just blended. Cook on hot, ungreased griddle until golden, flipping once.

Crêpes

Whip together 2 cups mix, 2 cups milk, and 4 eggs until smooth and lump-free. Cook on hot, greased crepe pan until golden, flipping once.

Waffles

Stir together 2 cups mix, 1½ cups milk, ½ cup oil, and 2 eggs (slightly beaten). Bake in a hot, sprayed waffle iron until golden.

Gravy Mix

This gravy mix yields 2 cups of wonderful gravy without any preservatives or food colorings—and at approximately a quarter the price of store-bought gravy mixes and canned gravies!

Ingredients	Quantity	12X Quantity
Flour	⅓ cup	4 cups
Beef or chicken soup base (see *Bouillon*, page 183)	5 teaspoons	1 cup
Parsley flakes	1 tablespoon	⅔ cup
Dried chives	2 teaspoons	½ cup
Thyme	⅛ teaspoon	1 teaspoon
Pepper	⅛ teaspoon	½ teaspoon
Yield (dry mix)	⅓ cup	4 cups

Combine all ingredients and store in a moistureproof, airtight container at room temperature until needed.

Use instructions:

Dry mix	⅓ cup	
Water	2 cups	
Yield (gravy)	2 cups	

Combine the gravy mix with 1 cup of the water. Set aside. In a saucepan over medium heat, bring the other cup of water to boiling and gradually stir the gravy mixture into the water. Continue stirring until it thickens.

Note: If you combine the gravy mix with cool water and then stir *constantly* while adding it to the hot water, you will always have smooth, lump-free gravy.

White Sauce Mix

Keep some of this mix on hand and you will be ready to create something stunning out of anything you have on hand.

Ingredients	Quantity	5X Quantity
Nonfat dry milk powder	⅓ cup	1½ cups
Flour	3 tablespoons	¾ cup
Salt	Sprinkle	1 teaspoon
Shortening (butter-flavored is best)	1 tablespoon	½ cup
Yield (dry mix)	½ cup	2½ cups

Combine all dry ingredients; cut in shortening. Store in moisture-proof, airtight container at room temperature for up to 6 months.

Use instructions: Combine all ingredients for desired sauce as shown below. Cook over medium heat, stirring constantly, or in the microwave on high for 5 minutes, stirring vigorously after each 45-second interval, just until thickened.

Select One:

Thin white sauce: 1 cup water plus ⅛ cup mix
Medium white sauce: 1 cup water plus ½ cup mix
Thick white sauce: 1 cup water plus ⅔ cup mix

Serve as White Sauce or Proceed with One of the Following:

Cheese Sauce

Make desired white sauce, then add ¼ teaspoon dry mustard plus 1 cup shredded Cheddar cheese.

Curry Sauce

Make desired white sauce, then add ⅛ teaspoon pepper, ⅛ teaspoon paprika, 1 teaspoon onion salt, 1 teaspoon curry powder, ⅛ teaspoon ginger, and then add 1 teaspoon lemon juice just before serving.

Béchamel

Make desired white sauce, substituting 1 cup of broth (see page 75) for the cup of water (blend with the dry mix). Add ⅛ teaspoon paprika.

Mornay

Make desired white sauce, then add ¼ cup Parmesan cheese, stirring until melted and smooth.

Guacamole Seasoning Mix

This mix costs less than 2¢ per teaspoon. Compare that to the commercial mixes offered in your supermarket!

Ingredients	Quantity	4X Quantity
Sugar	½ teaspoon	2 teaspoons
Salt	¼ teaspoon	1 teaspoon
Garlic powder	⅛ teaspoon	½ teaspoon
Cayenne	2 sprinkles	⅛ teaspoon
Yield (dry mix)	1 teaspoon	¼ cup

Combine all ingredients and store indefinitely in a moistureproof, airtight container at room temperature.

Use instructions:

Dry mix	1 teaspoon
Avocado, mashed (about 1 avocado)	½ cup
Sour cream	⅓ cup
Yield (guacamole dip)	⅔ cup

Combine all ingredients and mix well. Chill until ready to serve. If chilled for longer than a few hours, a harmless dark film will form over the surface of the dip. Simply skim it off, stir well, and serve. This guacamole keeps in refrigerator for up to 1 week.

Taco Seasoning Mix

This dry mix contains about 5¢ worth of ingredients, and makes tacos easy, quick, and reasonable!

Ingredients	Quantity	_X Quantity
Paprika	¼ teaspoon	
Onion flakes	2 teaspoons	
Chili powder	1 teaspoon	
Cornstarch	½ teaspoon	
Garlic salt	1 teaspoon	
Oregano flakes	¼ teaspoon	
Cumin	½ teaspoon	
Yield (dry mix)	3 tablespoons	

Mix all ingredients and store indefinitely in a moistureproof, airtight container at room temperature.

Use instructions:

Dry mix	1½ tablespoons
Water	½ cup
Ground beef	1 pound
Yield	6 servings

Stir the dry mix into the water. Brown the ground beef, then add the combined water and dry mix. Simmer for about 15 minutes, stirring occasionally. Serve with other favorite taco fixings or use in any recipe calling for taco meat.

Pizza Seasoning Mix

If pizza is as popular at your house as I think it is, you will love the pizza parlor flavor this recipe affords for mere pennies.

Ingredients	Quantity	12X Quantity
Onion flakes	½ teaspoon	2 tablespoons
Crushed red pepper	½ teaspoon	2 tablespoons
Oregano flakes	¼ teaspoon	1 tablespoon
Parsley flakes	¼ teaspoon	1 tablespoon
Basil	⅛ teaspoon	2 teaspoons
Garlic powder	⅛ teaspoon	2 teaspoons
Salt	⅛ teaspoon	2 teaspoons
Dill weed	Sprinkle	½ teaspoon
Pepper	Sprinkle	½ teaspoon
Yield (dry mix)	2 teaspoons	½ cup

Combine all ingredients and store indefinitely in a moistureproof, airtight container at room temperature.

Use instructions: Use in any recipe calling for pizza seasoning mix, or combine 2 teaspoons of the mix with 8 ounces tomato sauce and assemble pizza as usual.

Spaghetti Sauce Seasoning Mix

Whether it's spaghetti, lasagne, or marinara sauce you need, you will enjoy the convenience and taste of this recipe for a fraction of the store-bought cost.

Ingredients	Quantity	_X Quantity
Onion flakes	1 tablespoon	
Garlic powder	1 teaspoon	
Salt	1 teaspoon	
Oregano flakes	¼ teaspoon	
Thyme	¼ teaspoon	
Pepper	⅛ teaspoon	
Yield (dry mix)	1 tablespoon	

Combine all ingredients and store in a moistureproof, airtight container at room temperature until needed.

Use instructions:

Dry mix	1 tablespoon	
Tomato sauce	15 ounces	
Olive oil	1 teaspoon	
Yield (sauce)	2 cups	

Combine all ingredients in a saucepan over medium heat; bring to a boil, reduce heat, and simmer for 20 minutes or longer. Stir occasionally.

Shake-and-Bake Meat Breading Mix

This combination is easy to assemble and helps the busy cook make something special in a hurry. You won't miss paying the high price of commercial coating, either.

Ingredients	Quantity	_X Quantity
Basil	2 teaspoons	
Dry bread crumbs	4 cups	
Celery salt	1 tablespoon	
Garlic powder	1 teaspoon	
Paprika	1 tablespoon	
Pepper	1 tablespoon	
Salt	2 teaspoons	
Yield (coating mix)	4 cups	

Combine all ingredients and store in a moistureproof, airtight container at room temperature for up to 6 months.

Use instructions:

Chicken

Combine 1 cup mix with ½ teaspoon sage plus ½ teaspoon thyme in a gallon-size plastic bag. Shake cut-up chicken pieces in the combination and arrange in ungreased baking dishes. Bake at 350°F for 1¼ hours, turning once during cooking period.

Beef or Veal

Combine 1 cup mix with ½ teaspoon oregano flakes in a gallon-size plastic bag. Shake individual steaks in combination and bake on greased baking sheets for 1 hour at 300°F.

Pork

Combine 1 cup mix with ¼ teaspoon allspice in a gallon-size plastic bag. Shake individual chops in the mixture and bake on ungreased baking sheets at 350°F for 45 minutes.

Meat Loaf Seasoning Mix

Ingredients	Quantity	_X Quantity
Oatmeal or bread crumbs	4 cups	
Garlic powder	1 teaspoon	
Onion flakes	½ cup	
Nonfat dry milk powder	¾ cup	
Onion soup base (see *Bouillon*, page 183)	¼ cup	
Oregano flakes	1 tablespoon	
Parsley flakes	⅓ cup	
Pepper	1 teaspoon	
Yield (seasoning mix)	4½ cups	

Combine all ingredients and store in a moistureproof, airtight container at room temperature until needed.

Use instructions:

Dry mix	1½ cups	
Ground beef	2 pounds	
Cold water	⅔ cup	
Egg, lightly beaten	1	
Yield (meat loaf)	1	

Combine all ingredients and form into a loaf. Glaze with catsup or other favorite topping and bake at 350°F for 1¼ hours. Drain fat, let stand for 10 minutes, slice, and serve.

Instant Hot Cocoa Mix

Those little envelopes from Switzerland can dent your food budget. Replace them with this excellent and domestic-priced combination.

Ingredients	Quantity	8X Quantity
Nonfat dry milk powder	1⅓ cups	10⅔ cups
Hershey's Chocolate Quik	2 tablespoons	2 cups
Powdered coffee creamer	1 tablespoon	6 ounces
Powdered sugar	1½ tablespoons	¾ cup
Yield (dry mix)	1½ cups	11 cups

Combine all ingredients and store in a moistureproof, airtight container at room temperature until needed.

Use instructions: Measure ½ cup cocoa mix into 1 cup hot water. Stir and serve.

Dried Beans Mix

Dried beans are a staple in many homes, and can be considered as a "dry mix" because they keep indefinitely in their dried state. They are a delicious, fat-free, cholesterol-free source of protein, and are much less expensive when you cook your own rather than use canned beans. If you are used to the canned variety, be aware that preparing your own beans takes several hours—and this is *before* they are ready to use in your favorite recipes.

The simplest, easiest way to cook beans is in an electric Crock-Pot. Just add water and beans in the ratios shown in the chart, set the Crock-Pot on High, and your beans will be ready to eat or use in recipes after 4 to 6 hours, depending on the type of bean and its age. By using a Crock-Pot, you can cook beans overnight or while you are at work—a real time-saver.

If you prefer the standard soaking method for cooking beans, place the beans in a large pot with enough water to cover them by half an inch or more. Allow beans to soak for several hours or overnight. Drain off the soaking water, then add fresh water in the ratio shown in the chart. Bring the water to a boil, then reduce heat and simmer, with the pot not quite covered, until the beans are tender but not mushy (see approximate cooking times in the chart).

Always remember to sort through and then rinse the beans before you soak them or put them in a Crock-Pot. And note that split peas and lentils do not require a presoaking; they cook very quickly.

Beans (1 cup dry)	Water	Cooking time (if presoaked)	Yield
Black beans	4 cups	1½ hours	2 cups
Black-eyed peas	3 cups	1 hour	2 cups
Chickpeas (garbanzos)	4 cups	3 hours	2 cups
Cowpeas	3 cups	30 minutes	2½ cups
Kidney beans	3 cups	1½ hours	2 cups
Lentils and split peas (no presoaking)	3 cups	30 to 40 minutes	2¼ cups
Lima beans	2 cups	1½ hours	1¼ cups
Navy beans or Great Northern beans	3½ cups	2¼ hours	2 cups

Beans (1 cup dry)	Water	Cooking time (if presoaked)	Yield
Pinto (pink) beans	3 cups	2½ hours	2 cups
Red beans	3 cups	3 hours	2 cups
Soybeans	4 cups	3 or more hours	2 cups

See also: *Refried beans* (page 209).

7.

Simple Side Dishes

Fruit, vegetable, and grain side dishes taste great, add variety to our menus, and provide vitamins, minerals, and roughage that our bodies need. In our rush to get dinner on the table we sometimes forget the importance of serving all three of these dietary components with each meal. If we do remember, we often opt for the advertised "easy" side dishes that come buried under high-calorie and high-sodium sauces.

My husband is an avid and creative gardener who enjoys watching our backyard, weed-free plot bring forth fruit in its season. Because of his garden, we have fresh produce during middle to late summer and we are able to freeze any excess for the winter months. I use my mother's old pressure canner to put up pears and peaches that I buy in bulk when the prices are lowest, and we also pick berries and freeze any that escape immediate consumption. In other words, we are blessed with the freshest, healthiest, and most tasty produce available.

If your situation does not offer the option of homegrown goodness, you can still enjoy fresh fruits and vegetables by taking advantage of seasonal values. Use the chart on pages 95–96 to help you plan the produce portion of your menu. You might even want to copy it and add it as a separate page to your Kitchen Notebook. Start watching the seasonal values in your area and make notes on your chart so you know which week to start watching for bargain buys.

Take advantage of farmers' markets, roadside stands, and produce department sales. Some warehouse clubs offer bulk purchase produce for large families or for those willing to do the work of preserving it at home.

SEASONAL GUIDE TO FRUITS AND VEGETABLES

PRODUCE ITEM	BEST MONTH(S) TO BUY					
	Jan/Feb	Mar/April	May/June	July/Aug	Sept/Oct	Nov/Dec
Fruit:						
Apples	X	X			X	X
Avocados	X	X	X		X	X
Bananas	X	X	X	X	X	X
Blueberries			X	X		
Cherries			X	X		
Grapes				X	X	X
Grapefruit	X	X	X			X
Lemons			X	X	X	
Limes			X	X	X	
Melons	X	X	X			
Oranges	X	X	X	X	X	
Peaches			X	X	X	
Pears				X	X	X
Pineapple		X	X	X		
Plums			X	X	X	
Raspberries		X	X	X		
Strawberries		X	X	X		

PRODUCE ITEM	BEST MONTH(S) TO BUY					
	Jan/Feb	Mar/April	May/June	July/Aug	Sept/Oct	Nov/Dec
Vegetables:						
Beans			X	X		
Broccoli	X				X	X
Brussels sprouts	X				X	X
Carrots	X	X	X	X	X	X
Corn				X	X	X
Cucumber			X	X		
Eggplant				X	X	
Lettuce	X	X	X	X	X	X
Peas	X	X	X	X		
Peppers			X	X	X	
Potatoes	X	X	X	X	X	X
Spinach	X	X				
Summer squash			X	X	X	
Sweet potatoes					X	X
Tomato			X	X		
Winter squash					X	X

During produce slumps, choose a variety of sale-priced fruits and vegetables and then fill in with a selection from the frozen foods department. If you want to avoid the time-consuming, expensive, and high-calorie toppings and sauces frequently accompanying side dishes, simply avoid buying fruits and vegetables in tin cans. The taste difference will convince you to serve them in a way that features their natural goodness.

I make exceptions to the above no-tin-can rule when it comes to buying pineapple, mandarin oranges, and fruit cocktail. Canned vegetables that I purchase include olives, mushrooms, chop suey vegetables, bean sprouts, kidney beans, baked beans, and tomato pastes and sauces. When these go on sale, I stock up.

Meeting our fruit intake requirements usually includes eating fresh fruits either whole, sliced, or sectioned, drinking fruit juices or fruit whips from fresh or frozen juice concentrates, enjoying Frosty Fruit Cups (see page 55), and an occasional topped fruit salad. A few of my favorite, quick-and-easy fruit side recipes begin on page 103.

While we do enjoy special recipes on occasion, if you were to stop by our home at mealtime on most days, you would probably find plain fruit being served in small glass dessert dishes set to the upper left of each place setting. Fruit is simply delicious.

Likewise, vegetables are presented either raw or cooked until tender-crisp and then served without sauces. To encourage children to eat more vegetables, serve mixed vegetables, still frozen, right out of the bag. Raw vegetables and Dill Dip (page 172) are also a favorite.

If you are looking for an additional way to serve veggies, save money by making your own Tempura Batter (page 110) or Onion Rings (page 111).

On rare occasions we indulge and serve vegetables with white, cheese, or mornay sauce (recipes on pages 82–83). Of course, the easiest topping, if you don't mind the calories, is melted margarine or butter. Another favorite is my inexpensive version of Cheez Whiz (page 107) and a quick-fix hollandaise sauce (page 109).

Frequently, the need to prepare vegetable side dishes is eliminated by their inclusion in the main dish. Serving Chinese dishes (chow mein, stir-fry, etc.) and Mexican meals (tacos, taco salads, etc.) on a regular basis offers taste, convenience, and economy.

Pinch Hitting

As for starch side dishes, you need not have potatoes, rice, or noodles on hand in order to serve dinner. Consider serving corn bread, muffins, or toast as a side dish. Make stuffing or serve split buns topped with your main entrée—this works great with meat and gravy dishes. Remember, every trip to the store is costly in both time and money. Use what you have on hand whenever possible.

Popular Potato Pleasers

Potatoes are undoubtedly the most loved and the most versatile of all
the vegetables. They offer great taste and are inexpensive while serving as both a vegetable and starch side dish. Unfortunately, potatoes
do not thaw well once frozen, and thus require preparation prior to
each meal. To scrub potatoes, invest in a heavy-duty pan scrubber, the
kind with metal bristles and a handle. Instead of peeling or wasting
time with regular vegetable scrubbers, these little brushes get the job
done quickly. Use the following potato ideas to reduce the time or
money you are investing in packages of dried-out, vitamin-stripped
potato side dishes. The overpriced, high-sodium boxed potatoes can
be replaced for a few pennies.

Oven-Baked

Scrub potatoes under running water with heavy-duty scrubber, poke
with a fork and place on oven rack. These can cook with your other
dinner components at virtually any temperature as long as you allow
at least 60 minutes. If by themselves, bake at 350°F for 50 minutes.
Serve plain or with butter, gravy, sour cream, or yogurt.

Microwave-Baked

Scrub and poke potatoes with a fork. Microwave on high for 6 minutes for the first potato and 3 minutes for each additional potato. Rotate potatoes a few times during cooking period. Squeeze or poke
with fork to determine doneness.

Oven Hash Browns

Beginning with partially cooked potatoes, slip the skins off as you
grate the potatoes over a greased jelly roll pan. If using freshly baked
(hot) potatoes, wear rubber gloves. Bake grated potatoes in 425°F

oven for about 20 minutes, until golden brown on top. Add salt and pepper to taste and serve hot.

Potato Chippers

If you crave potato chips but can't afford the 1 gram of fat per potato chip, peel one potato and then thinly slice it using a potato peeler. Generously salt a microwave-safe baking dish and arrange potato slices in a single layer around the outside edges. Microwave on high until slightly bubbled and sizzling (3 to 6 minutes). Slices should be totally crisped but not brown. Remove chips with a spatula as they reach doneness, and eat them fresh or store them in a zip-top bag for later. Note: If these are overcooked they taste awful. Remove any "early" chips as soon as they are cooked.

Rendezvous with Rice

Create your own side-dish specialties with versatile rice and whatever vegetables are on hand.

Oven-Baked: Bake 2 cups rice in a moderate oven with other dinner components for a minimum of 30 minutes as follows: 2 cups rice covered with 5 cups boiling water or broth, 1 teaspoon salt (omit if using broth), and 2 tablespoons margarine.

Stove-Top: Bring 4 cups water to a boil then add 2 cups rice. Cover tight, reduce heat, and simmer for 20 minutes without removing lid.

Variations:

- Add 2 tablespoons onion soup base to 4 cups boiling water before adding 2 cups rice, then proceed as above.

- Add 2 tablespoons beef soup base and 1 teaspoon tomato paste to 4 cups boiling water before adding 2 cups rice. Proceed as above.

- Add 2 tablespoons chicken soup base plus 1 teaspoon parsley flakes to 4 cups boiling water before adding 2 cups rice. Proceed as above.

- Add 1 tablespoon chopped parsley and 2 tablespoons melted margarine just before serving 4 cups cooked rice.

- Stir ¼ cup roasted almonds or cashews and 2 tablespoons melted margarine into the cooked rice just before serving.

- Sauté ¼ pound mushrooms in 2 tablespoons butter and blend into cooked rice just before serving.

- Blend 1 raw shredded carrot and 2 teaspoons parsley flakes into cooked rice. Cover and let stand for 5 minutes before serving.

- Add ½ cup cooked, drained vegetables (peas, carrots, broccoli, etc.) just before serving.

■ Top cooked rice with 1½ cups of your favorite sauce (see page 82 for white sauce and variations or page 81 for gravy mixes).

Cook Ahead: Cook rice as usual, without removing the lid. Leave undisturbed and still tightly covered for up to 20 minutes. Fluff with a fork (and add perk-ups if desired) just before serving.

Noodle Perk-Ups

With the noodle side dish options that follow, you can spend less and enjoy every bite. Watch for price bargains on angel hair, wide, and spaghetti noodles, then stock up because dried pastas last indefinitely if stored in a cool, dry place. The only boxed, bagged, canned, or frozen pasta combinations that do not feel like highway robbery are bargain-priced macaroni and cheese and ramen noodles. Take heart—you really can eat better than ever without spending hours over a hot stove!

Cook 8 ounces noodles (macaroni, spaghetti, angel hair, egg, etc.) as directed on package. Drain, rinse, and perk up as follows:

- Place pasta in ovenproof serving dish and crumble corn flakes, tortilla chips, potato chips, corn chips, or shredded cheese on top. Place under broiler for 1 to 2 minutes until cheese is sizzling.

- Stir in ⅓ cup Parmesan cheese and ⅓ cup whipped topping for a rich Fettuccine Alfredo. Garnish with bacon bits if desired.

- Combine 2 teaspoons olive oil, ½ cup sliced black or green olives, and 1 teaspoon garlic salt. Stir combination into cooked noodles until well mixed.

- Add 1 cup cooked, drained peas, broccoli, spinach, or mixed vegetables. Toss and serve.

- Pour 1½ cups of your favorite sauce on top (sauce recipe ideas are on page 82).

Fruit Toppings and Dips

Honey Syrup

Simply heat some honey in the microwave for a few seconds and pour a few tablespoons over the fruit you have on hand; stir to coat and serve. Yum.

Tangy Fruit Topping

1 cup mayonnaise*
1 cup whipped topping*

Whisk together and serve over any fruit combination.

Apple Dip

7-ounce jar marshmallow cream
8 ounces cream cheese*
1 teaspoon vanilla

Blend until smooth and serve as a dip.

Whipped Dressing

1 cup whipped topping*
1 teaspoon sugar
½ teaspoon mustard
½ teaspoon vanilla

Fold together and serve over any fruit combination. Yields a rich, cream cheese flavor.

* May be replaced with a fat-reduced alternative.

Frosty Fruit Drinks

1 6-ounce can frozen fruit juice concentrate (orange, apple, etc.) or 2 cups fresh or frozen, thawed fruit (berries, bananas, etc.)

1 cup milk

1 cup water (eliminate when using fresh or frozen fruit)

½ cup sugar or ⅓ cup honey (reduce to ¼ cup sugar or 2½ tablespoons honey when using fruit)

1 teaspoon vanilla

8 ice cubes

Yield (4 servings)

Combine desired ingredients in blender container and whir on high until slushy. Serve immediately.

Applesauce

Substitute this recipe for prepared, jarred applesauce.

Ingredients	Quantity	5X Quantity
Apples, peeled, cored, and sliced	2 pounds	10 pounds
Water	½ cup	2 cups
Cinnamon	⅛ teaspoon	¼ teaspoon
Ground cloves	⅛ teaspoon	¼ teaspoon
Sugar	⅓ cup	1 cup
Yield	2 cups	10 cups

Combine the apple slices, water, and spices in a saucepan and bring to a boil. Reduce heat, cover, and simmer for 10 minutes, or until soft; stir until smooth. Add the sugar and stir well. Cool completely and store in the refrigerator for up to 6 weeks. Or preserve according to standard preserving guidelines.

Watergate Salad

The delicatessen version of this party salad is very expensive.

Ingredients	Quantity	_X Quantity
Pistachio pudding mix	1 3-ounce box	
Pineapple, crushed	14 ounces	
Mini-marshmallows	1 cup	
Bananas (optional)	3	
Whipped topping	8 ounces	
Yield	6 to 8 servings	

Mix dry pudding powder with pineapple, including juice. Add marsh-mallows and sliced bananas; fold in whipped topping. Refrigerate until ready to serve. Tastes as good immediately as it does 3 days later.

Cheese Whiz

Whether it is the high price or the high fat content that causes you to moan when reaching for this convenient food at the dairy case, this recipe offers a 40 percent cost savings without much effort.

Ingredients	Quantity	Quantity for low-fat version
American or Cheddar cheese	8 ounces	—
Defatted American or Cheddar cheese	—	8 ounces
Butter	2 tablespoons	—
Sugar	½ tablespoon	1 teaspoon
Nonfat cottage cheese	—	4 ounces
Milk	½ cup	—
Liquid nonfat milk	—	1 teaspoon
Prepared mustard	½ teaspoon	½ teaspoon
Yield	1 cup, for a total of 1,173 calories/97 grams fat	1 cup, for a total of 499 calories/17.6 grams fat

Cube or crumble cheese. Combine all ingredients in a microwave-safe dish and microwave on high for 1 to 2 minutes, stirring vigorously after each 30-second interval, until melted and smooth. Add milk, as needed, to achieve desired consistency. Store in an airtight container in refrigerator for up to 3 months.

Mayonnaise

When the recipe requires real mayo, nothing tastes as good or costs less (approximately $1 per recipe) than this sensational spread.

Ingredients	Quantity	2X Quantity
Eggs	2	4
Lemon juice	1 tablespoon	2 tablespoons
Sugar	2 teaspoons	4 teaspoons
Dry mustard	1 teaspoon	2 teaspoons
Salt	½ teaspoon	1 teaspoon
Crisco oil	2 cups	4 cups
Yield	2 cups	4 cups

Combine the eggs, lemon juice, sugar, mustard, salt, and ¼ cup of the oil in a blender container and whir on high until smooth. Add remaining oil very gradually in a slow, steady stream through the center opening, blending until all oil is absorbed. Store in a glass jar in the refrigerator until needed.

Note: I experimented with many mayonnaise recipes before I found one that was quick, easy, rich-tasting, and practically foolproof. This recipe works like a charm every time and requires only 3 minutes to assemble.

Hollandaise Sauce

Ingredients	Quantity	_X Quantity
Sour cream	¼ cup	
Mayonnaise	¼ cup	
Lemon juice	1 teaspoon	
Prepared mustard	½ teaspoon	
Yield	½ cup	

Combine all ingredients and blend well. Heat and serve over vegetables or baked or broiled meat.

Variations

Fat Free

Substitute fat-free sour cream and fat-free salad dressing for an excellent sauce without guilt.

Béarnaise

Add ⅛ teaspoon tarragon and serve over meat, fish, or vegetables.

Choron

Add 2 tablespoons tomato paste and serve with eggs or meatloaf.

Maltaise

Add 1 tablespoon grated orange peel and 2 tablespoons orange juice and serve with fish or vegetables.

Tempura Batter

Ingredients	Quantity	_X Quantity
Flour	1 cup	
Baking Soda	½ teaspoon	
Salt	¼ teaspoon	
Water	⅓ to ½ cup	
Eggs	2	
Cooking oil	1 tablespoon plus enough for frying	
Yield	2½ cups batter	

Combine dry ingredients; make a well and pour in remaining ingredients. Stir gently until just blended. Set aside for 20 minutes. Dip raw or thawed, washed, and dried bite-size vegetable pieces into batter. Allow excess to drip off, then fry in hot oil until puffed and golden. Test first vegetable to be sure it is cooked through, note frying time, and proceed with remaining vegetables.

Onion Ring Batter Mix

Onion rings are always popular, and they taste great fresh or reheated from frozen.

Ingredients	Quantity	8X Quantity
Flour	1½ cups	12 cups
Nonfat dry milk powder	2 tablespoons	1 cup
Salt	1½ teaspoons	4 tablespoons
Yield (dry mix)	1½ cups	12 cups

Combine and store indefinitely in a moistureproof, airtight container at room temperature.

Use instructions:

Dry mix	1½ cups
Hot tap water	1¼ cups
Cooking oil	3 tablespoons plus extra for frying
Onions	4 to 6
Yield (onion rings)	100+

Combine dry mix, water, and oil; set aside for at least 15 minutes and for up to 2 hours. Slice onions and pull apart rings. Heat 2 inches of oil to 425°F. Dip each onion ring into batter, let excess drip off, and deep-fry rings for 2 to 4 minutes, until golden brown. Cool and drain on paper towels; sprinkle with salt. Serve hot or place on cookie sheets in freezer until frozen; slip frozen rings into freezer-quality zip-top bags and store until needed.

To prepare from frozen, remove as many onion rings as desired to an ungreased baking sheet. Heat oven to 400°F and recrisp frozen rings for 10 to 15 minutes, until heated through. Serve hot.

8.

What to Serve
When Company's Coming

Being on a tight budget need not limit your hosting opportunities. Even though my husband and I do quite a bit of entertaining, we maintain a 50¢ per-person-per-meal budget. Since Dave will sometimes bring home business associates without warning me (I am fine with this!), I usually view shared meals as expanded or embellished family meals. I cover up my $45 junk shop table with an inexpensive lace tablecloth and serve food in the prettiest dishes I have. Abiding by proper table-setting etiquette brings out the best in my stoneware dishes, inexpensive silverware, and glasses. Cloth napkins add a softer touch and a lot of class to an otherwise simple affair. They cost a few bucks up front, but are well worth it because they last for years.

I rely on pretty serving bowls, platters, and pitchers to dress up the table. Thrift shops almost always have at least a meager selection of used crystal and glass dishes available at reasonable prices. Shop around a bit and you may be surprised at how fancy a table you can set for only a minimal investment.

A few years ago I came across some little cut-glass dessert cups at my local Ben Franklin store. These small dishes, which I purchased for under $1 each, are the perfect size for so many things—lettuce salads, fruit, ice cream, and so on. They are preferable to stemmed dessert glasses because they stack and therefore take less shelf space. Watch for a set at the thrift shop or your local five-and-ten.

Other pretty perks include serving molded butter or margarine, and lining a wicker basket with a napkin to serve warmed breads, biscuits, or muffins. Garnishes always add flair; try a sprig of parsley, a tomato wedge, or carrot curls. Even a thin slice of lemon twisted onto the rim of each glass of ice water adds class.

If you are most comfortable in jeans and a sweatshirt, invite friends for a barbecue or pizza party. Forget the fancy table settings and break out the potato chips! The reality is that good friends and good food are a great combination.

Many people prefer entertaining in restaurants and it is little wonder why. No cooking, no housecleaning, no washing dishes, and you get great tasting food in a nice setting. The only drawback is that it is relatively impersonal compared to dining in, and it costs a pretty penny. Just the other day I stopped by the local ice cream shop three blocks from home and purchased *small* snacks for six children. My total was $3.51. At home in my freezer I had a 24-pack of freeze pops on sticks that I purchased on sale for 79¢. I paid over 400 percent markup for this small service.

If the only thing holding you back from hosting a dinner party is the reality that there isn't time to prepare your home plus pull off a satisfactory meal, consider inviting friends for a shared meal. Probably one-third of the entertaining we do is in this fashion. We employ this practical entertaining style for brunches, dinners, and other parties (New Year's drop-ins for example). Each Christmas I host a drop-in ladies brunch—friends come and go for most of the day. I bake a few special dishes and arrange the table with some of my prettiest candies and cookies. Invitations include a note that reads "Bring a brunch item or a plate of Christmas goodies to share." The party is lots of fun and it's always interesting to taste everyone else's favorites.

We have found that people enjoy coming to the door with something in hand. Food is both practical and delicious. Besides, there are some people who would never accept an invitation unless we allowed them to help with the work.

If dropping big bucks at fine restaurants is a regular occurrence because of the culinary genius of a certain chef, consider checking with *Bon Appetit*'s R.S.V.P. Department. Readers are encouraged to send in requests for previously unpublished recipes from their favorite restaurants. If there is a dish that inspires you to pay in a big way, write to them at R.S.V.P., *Bon Appetit* magazine, 360 Madison Avenue, New York, NY 10017. Also, you might want to check with your library for back issues of the magazine.

Many of my favorite foods are takeoffs from the food industry's hottest sellers and most are easy to make at home. Hosting theme dinners (at which I provide all dinner components) is another favorite entertaining option. If you are in the mood for Mexican but are short on dinero for the restaurant route, begin your thrifty fiesta with the excellent Sopaipilla recipe on page 66, then make Burritos or Chimichangas (page 116) plus a terrific Mexican dessert (page 118).

Another Mexican favorite features our own Salsa (page 119) with a platter of nacho chips. We use the great tasting El GranDeli Nacho Tortilla Chips (tell your grocer they come from Bec-Lin Foods, Inc., Perham, MN 56573), which go on sale for less than half the cost of the leading brands. Place a single layer of the chips on a microwave-safe platter. Sprinkle with jalapeño peppers or black olives, then cover generously with shredded Cheddar (not mozzarella) cheese. Microwave on high for 90 seconds. Serve with lettuce, tomato, guacamole, and salsa.

If Mexican is too spicy, Chinese is an excellent option. I used to drive halfway across Minneapolis to pay $2.75 for a side order of four small pieces of Shrimp Toast. Since I couldn't buy them now if I wanted to (nobody in Warroad sells them), I came up with my own version (page 120) at a whopping 6¢ each! Other reasonable recreations can be found on pages 121–125. You can turn your kitchen into a Chinese restaurant anytime you like.

If you single-handedly support your local pizza shop, try any of the company-pleasing recipes on pages 126–129. If meat and potatoes are your preference, opt for barbecues (page 130) or glazed ham (page 131).

Finally, at a terrific cost savings over the ready-made grocery store price, children and adults will rave about homemade Corn Dogs (page 132). This recipe works well for mass production (one mess, many meals). Stock up when weiners drop to 50 percent of their regular price—usually around summer holiday weekends. Since both weiners and corn dogs freeze well, you can either freeze the hot dogs until you have time to cook them up as a big batch, or you can make them now, enjoy some for supper, and freeze the rest in serving-size, freezer-quality zip-top bags for later.

Consommé

If you enjoy serving consommé but your budget rejects the high price of the canned variety, indulge at less than half the cost.

Ingredients	Quantity	_X Quantity
Unflavored gelatin	1 teaspoon	
Water	2½ cups	
Beef or chicken soup base (see *Bouillon*, page 183)	4 teaspoons	
Tomato paste (for beef consommé only)	1 teaspoon	
Yield (20 ounces)	2 10-ounce cans	

Soften the gelatin in ½ cup cold water. Heat the remaining water over medium heat until boiling. Add the soup base, gelatin, and tomato paste (omit paste for chicken consommé). Continue heating, stirring constantly, until thickened. Cover and chill until ready to serve. (The consommé continues to thicken as it cools.)

To serve: Stir the consommé gently with the tines of a fork, then spoon into individual serving dishes. Garnish with parsley sprigs.

Note: I use consommé as a flavor booster in a variety of recipes. Since the thickening action provided by the gelatin is unnecessary, I omit the gelatin and combine the other ingredients, heating just until warmed through. This yields the appropriate flavors without wasting a packet of the gelatin.

Burritos/Chimichangas

Chimichangas are essentially fried burritos.

Burrito/Chimichanga Dry Seasoning Mix

Ingredients	Quantity	_X Quantity
Onion flakes	2 tablespoons	
Oregano flakes	1 teaspoon	
Ground cumin	¼ teaspoon	
Garlic powder	⅛ teaspoon	
Yield (dry mix)	2 tablespoons	

Combine dry ingredients and store in moistureproof, airtight container at room temperature until needed. Use following instructions or add 1 tablespoon vinegar and use as a replacement for prepackaged store-bought chimichanga seasoning mix.

Burrito/Chimichanga Filling

Dry mix	2 tablespoons
Ground beef, browned	1 cup
Tomato sauce	1 cup
Water	¼ cup
White vinegar	1 tablespoon
Yield (filling mix)	2 cups

Simmer ingredients for 15 to 20 minutes, stirring occasionally, until almost all of the moisture evaporates. Remove from heat and cool slightly or store in an airtight container in the fridge or freezer until needed.

Burritos

Filling mix	2 cups
Corn or flour tortillas	8 8-inch shells
Shredded Cheddar cheese	1 cup
Yield	8 burritos

Place tortilla shells on a microwave-safe dish and cover tightly with plastic wrap. Microwave on high for 1 minute. Remove the plastic and measure ¼ cup hot filling into the center of each tortilla and fold like an envelope. Cool and freeze for future use, or garnish with Cheddar cheese and other favorites such as sour cream, guacamole, shredded lettuce, or diced tomatoes, and serve hot.

Chimichangas

Filling mix	2 cups
Corn or flour tortillas	8 8-inch shells
Oil for frying	
Yield	8 chimichangas

Heat 1 inch of oil in skillet to 350°F. Measure ¼ cup filling into center of each tortilla, then fold like an envelope, securing with toothpicks. Fry for about 2 minutes, turn, and continue frying until golden brown. Remove to paper towels to drain. Cool and freeze or garnish as desired and serve hot.

From frozen: Place frozen chimichangas or burritos on a cookie sheet and lay a piece of aluminum foil loosely over top (to prevent overbrowning). Heat in 375°F oven for 20 to 25 minutes.

Fried Ice Cream Dessert— Mexican Style

Ingredients	Quantity	2X Quantity
Margarine or butter, melted	6 tablespoons	12 tablespoons
Brown sugar	¾ cup	1½ cups
Corn flakes, crushed	2 cups	4 cups
Coconut	⅓ cup	⅔ cup
Walnuts, chopped	⅓ cup	⅔ cup
Vanilla ice cream	4 cups	½ gallon
Yield (pan size)	8 by 8 inches	9 by 13 inches

Combine the margarine and brown sugar; mix in the corn flakes, coconut, and walnuts. Layer most of the crumb mixture on the bottom of pan. Spread ice cream evenly over top and sprinkle with remaining crumbs. Freeze. When ready to serve, cut into squares.

Optional: Drizzle hot fudge sauce over top.

Salsa

If you garden, this combination is pretty much free. If not, you will still come out far ahead of the fortune charged for a 16-ounce jar.

Ingredients	Quantity	_X Quantity
Green pepper	1	
Jalapeño peppers	2	
Onion	1–2	
Medium tomatoes (or canned whole tomatoes)	4 (32 ounces)	
Garlic powder	½ teaspoon	
Salt	½ teaspoon	
Lemon juice	2 tablespoons	
Yield	4 cups	

Finely dice peppers and onion. Peel the tomatoes and blend on high in a blender for 30 seconds. Combine all ingredients and stir (do not use blender). Store in an airtight container in refrigerator for up to 3 weeks or preserve in jars according to standard preserving guidelines.

Shrimp Toast

Ingredients	Quantity	_X Quantity
Oil for frying		
Flour	½ cup	
Cornstarch	2 tablespoons	
Salt	1 teaspoon	
Accent	1 teaspoon	
Sugar	½ teaspoon	
Ginger	¼ teaspoon	
Egg	1	
Oil	1 teaspoon	
Water	½ cup	
Tiny peeled shrimp	1 4-ounce can	
White bread	10 slices	
Yield	40 triangles	

Heat 2 inches of oil to 375°F. Combine dry ingredients, set aside. Combine egg, 1 teaspoon oil, water, and shrimp; stir well and then mix with dry ingredients. Slice each piece of bread into 4 equal triangles.

Place 1 bread triangle onto a metal spatula that you are holding in your good hand (right hand for right-handed people, etc.). Use your other hand to spoon some of the shrimp mixture onto the triangle, then immediately and carefully submerge it in the hot oil. Slip the spatula out from under the bread and repeat with additional triangles until first toast is ready to turn (it will be deep golden brown underneath and ready in less than 3 minutes). Turn it over and allow it to brown on the second side. Remove to a cooling rack that is covered with paper towels. Let drain while you fry the remaining toasts. Serve immediately or keep warm in 250°F oven for up to 45 minutes (door slightly ajar).

These freeze well and can be reheated in the oven from frozen. Place desired number on ungreased baking sheet and lay a piece of aluminum foil loosely over top. Bake at 400°F for 10 to 12 minutes until heated through.

Egg Rolls

These taste great at only 19¢ each!

Ingredients	Quantity	_X Quantity
Ground pork	1 pound	
Salt	½ teaspoon	
Cornstarch	½ teaspoon	
Soy sauce	½ teaspoon	
Green cabbage, finely shredded	1 head (approximately 2½ pounds)	
Oil	2 tablespoons	
Salt	1 teaspoon	
Five-spice powder	1 teaspoon	
Egg roll wrappers	1 pound	
Oil for frying		
Yield	24 egg rolls	

Combine pork, salt, cornstarch, and soy sauce; cover and refrigerate for 20 minutes. While waiting, blanch the cabbage in boiling water for 2 minutes; rinse immediately in cold water and drain well. Squeeze off excess liquid. Stir-fry pork combination in 2 tablespoons oil until no longer pink. Add cabbage, salt, and 5-spice powder; mix then cool. Roll ½ cup filling into each egg roll wrapper as shown in the illustration on the next page. Heat 2 inches of oil to 370°F and fry egg rolls, seam side down, until golden; turn and let fry until golden. Remove to paper-towel-covered cooling racks. Cool and freeze, or serve hot with soy sauce or Sweet 'N' Sour Sauce (page 125).

From frozen: Place frozen rolls on an ungreased baking sheet and lay a piece of aluminum foil loosely over top. Bake in 350°F oven for 20 minutes, or until heated through.

Note: Egg roll wrappers should be kept covered with a damp towel.

1. Place ½ cup filling just below the center of the egg roll wrapper.
2. Fold up the bottom edge.
3. Bring in the two outside corners.
4. Complete the "envelope" by dabbing water on the fourth corner before rolling the egg roll closed.

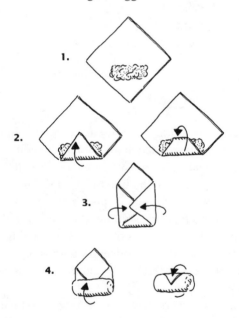

Chow Mein

Easy, inexpensive, low-fat, and delicious: What more could you ask?

Ingredients	Quantity	_X Quantity
Onion, diced	½ cup	
Celery, chopped	2 cups	
Water	1½ cups	
Chop suey vegetables or soybeans	1 14-ounce can	
Meat, cooked and cut up (leftover or stir-fried beef, chicken, or turkey)	1 cup	
Cornstarch	2 tablespoons	
Cold water	2 tablespoons	
Soy sauce	1 tablespoon	
Sugar	1 teaspoon	
Yield	4 servings	

Combine onion, celery, and water in a large saucepan; bring to a boil, reduce heat, and simmer for 10 minutes. Add vegetables and meat; cover and simmer for 5 minutes. In a small bowl, mix the cornstarch, cold water, soy sauce, and sugar. Pour into vegetable mixture, stirring constantly until thickened (about 2 minutes). Serve immediately over rice or let simmer, stirring occasionally, until ready to serve.

Fried Rice

Ingredients	Quantity	_X Quantity
Uncooked rice	⅔ cup	
Onion, chopped	1 medium	
Celery, chopped	2 stalks	
Oil	2 tablespoons	
Boiling water	1½ cups	
Beef or chicken soup base (see *Bouillon,* page 183)	1 tablespoon	
Soy sauce	2 tablespoons	
Cooked pork, chicken, or tiny shrimp, diced	1½ cups	
Yield	4 servings	

Cook and stir rice, onion, and celery in hot oil until rice is golden brown and onion is tender. Stir in remaining ingredients; heat to boiling. Lower heat, cover tightly, and simmer for 15 minutes without removing lid. Remove from heat and fluff with a fork. Cover and let stand for an additional 10 minutes. Serve hot.

Sweet 'N' Sour Sauce

You can pay the price for Chinese takeout, pay the price for the jarred variety at your local market, or pocket the profits and make it yourself for about 50¢ per recipe.

Ingredients	Quantity	_X Quantity
Pineapple juice	½ cup	
Catsup	½ cup	
Honey	3 tablespoons	
Water	2 tablespoons	
Vinegar	1 tablespoon	
Cornstarch	4 teaspoons	
Mustard	1 teaspoon	
Salt	¼ teaspoon	
Yield	1 cup	

Combine all ingredients in a microwave-safe dish and stir well. Microwave on high for 3½ minutes, stirring every 30 seconds, until thick and smooth.

Italian Cheese Loaf

Yep! This tastes just like the expensive restaurant version.

Cut an 11-inch loaf of Italian bread (from bakery or see recipe on page 155) in half as for a sandwich. Smother top and bottom halves with Italian Butter (recipe follows). Top liberally with mozzarella cheese and sprinkle with oregano and Parmesan. Place on a baking sheet and broil until cheese is slightly browned and bubbly. Slice and serve.

Italian Butter

Ingredients	Quantity	_X Quantity
Margarine, room temperature	¼ pound	
Garlic powder	2 teaspoons	
Onion salt	1 teaspoon	
Parsley flakes	1 teaspoon	
Yield	8 tablespoons	

Whip all ingredients together.

Italian Buttered Bread Strips

No Italian bread in the house? Toast slices of regular bread in toaster, then layer top with Italian Butter. Heat, buttered side up, under broiler for 2 minutes until sizzly. Slice into strips and serve hot.

Pesto

This authentic Italian taste goes together quickly and costs only a fraction of the specialty shop variety.

Ingredients	Quantity	_X Quantity
Olive oil	½ cup	
Parmesan	⅓ cup	
Chopped walnuts	2 tablespoons	
Garlic powder	1 tablespoon	
Basil	1 teaspoon	
Parsley flakes	1 teaspoon	
Yield	⅔ cup	

Combine ingredients in a blender and whir until smooth. Serve over spaghetti or pour into a glass jar and cover with a thin layer of olive oil. When ready to use, pour off the oil, and measure out needed amount (usually 2 to 3 tablespoons per recipe). Cover remaining pesto with same oil and return to the refrigerator for up to 8 months or freeze for up to 1 year. If you freeze pesto in ice cube trays, it's easy to snap out a single portion whenever you need it.

Deep-Dish Pizza Dough

In our supermarket a prepackaged deep-dish pizza dough without any toppings sells for ten times the cost of this quick-and-easy recipe.

Ingredients	Quantity	Do not expand
Yeast	1 tablespoon	
Flour	2½ cups	
Sugar	1 teaspoon	
Salt	1 teaspoon	
Warm (105–115°F) water	¾ cup	
Oil	2 tablespoons	
Yield (pan size)	1 10- to 12-inch pizza base	

Mix dry ingredients together with a fork; add water and oil all at once, stirring only until dough forms (do not worry if a bit of flour remains in bowl). Let rest at room temperature for 5 minutes. Spread dough onto a greased pizza pan and top with 8 ounces pizza sauce plus additional toppings as desired. Freeze for future use or bake for 20 minutes at 425°F, or until cheese is melted and bubbly.

   Note: To make additional deep-dish pizza crust, measure individual recipes out into separate bowls.

---

* Pizza Seasoning Mix recipe appears on page 86.

Italian Lasagne

This dish is easy, affordable, and low in fat if you opt for nonfat cheeses.

Ingredients	Quantity	_X Quantity
Ground beef, browned	1 pound	
Spaghetti Sauce Seasoning Mix (page 87)	1 package (2 tablespoons)	
Tomato sauce	30 ounces	
Cottage cheese	16 ounces	
Lasagne noodles, uncooked	8 ounces	
Parmesan cheese	½ cup	
Mozzarella cheese	8 ounces	
Cheddar cheese	4 ounces	
Yield (pan size)	1 9 by 13-inch pan	

Combine cooked ground beef, spice mix, and tomato sauce. Spread 1 cup of this combination in an ungreased baking dish. Layer a third of the noodles, Parmesan cheese, and mozzarella cheese, then repeat, starting again with beef mixture, until all are used up. Pour ½ cup water around sides of pan and cover tightly with aluminum foil. Freeze for later, or bake for 1 hour at 350°F, sprinkle with Cheddar cheese, and let stand for 20 minutes. Just before serving, place under broiler until cheese is bubbly.

From frozen: Place tightly covered pan (still frozen) in cold oven. Turn the oven to 350°F and let lasagne bake for 90 minutes. Remove to counter and sprinkle with Cheddar cheese. Let stand for 20 minutes, then place under broiler until cheese is bubbly.

Barbecue Sauce

Tastes great and goes together in a jiffy.

Ingredients	Quantity	_X Quantity
Catsup	½ cup	
Brown sugar	¼ cup	
Liquid smoke	¼ teaspoon	
Garlic powder	¼ teaspoon	
Yield	½ cup	

Combine all ingredients and brush over meat frequently during cooking period; or mix with 1 pound browned ground beef or leftover turkey meat and serve on buns.

Thick and Zesty Barbecue Sauce

Costs half of its famous store-bought equivalent.

Ingredients	Quantity	_X Quantity
Mayonnaise	1 cup	
Catsup	1 cup	
Worcestershire sauce	½ cup	
Brown sugar	½ cup	
Chili powder	⅓ cup	
Garlic powder	1 teaspoon	
Tabasco sauce	¼ teaspoon	
Yield	2½ cups	

Whisk ingredients together and brush onto meat frequently during cooking period. Store remaining sauce in an airtight container in the refrigerator for up to 6 months.

Ham Glaze

Ham is irresistible when baked in this glaze.

Ingredients	Quantity	_X Quantity
Brown sugar	1½ cups	
Flour	3 tablespoons	
Dry mustard	1 teaspoon	
Cinnamon	½ teaspoon	
Yield (dry mix)	1½ cups	

Combine all ingredients and store indefinitely in a moistureproof, airtight container at room temperature.

Use instructions:

Dry mix	½ cup
Water	2 tablespoons
Ham slices	8 to 10
Yield	4 to 5 servings

Place ham slices in a baking dish and spoon glaze over the top. Cover and bake at 350°F for 1 hour.

Corn Dogs on a Stick

Ingredients	Quantity	3X Quantity	8X Quantity
Salt	⅛ teaspoon	¼ teaspoon	½ teaspoon
Sugar	5 teaspoons	¼ cup	½ cup
Flour	½ cup	1½ cups	4 cups
Cornmeal	3 tablespoons	½ cup	1¼ cups
Baking powder	1 teaspoon	2 teaspoons	5 teaspoons
Eggs	1	2	6
Milk	⅓ cup	1 cup	2⅔ cups
Wieners and Popsicle sticks	10	30	80
Oil for frying			
Yield (corn dogs)	10	30	80

Combine salt, sugar, flour, cornmeal, and baking powder and mix with fork; add eggs and milk and stir until just moistened. Let stand for 30 minutes while you put sticks in the dogs and heat 3 inches of oil to 385°F. Pour part of the batter into a tall (32-ounce or so) beverage glass and dip the dogs, one at a time, covering completely. Allow the excess batter to drip off; slide the wiener into the oil. Fill the fryer with a single layer of corn dogs and cook for 2 to 3 minutes per side. Remove when golden and drain on a paper-towel-covered rack. Continue until all are fried. Serve hot or cool and freeze in family-size servings.

Kid-pleasin' idea: Since little ones like holding the stick almost as much as eating the corn dog, cut a few wieners in half, stick the half dogs, and proceed as if they were whole.

The Money-Saving Menu Rotation Plan

Opportunities to "drive through" and lose are on every corner. When you are tired and hungry, the only thing that will keep you on the straight and narrow is the assurance that something easy and appealing awaits you at home. At moments like these, the realization that you are paying upward of thirty dollars an hour for someone else to assemble your burgers and fries is only slightly convincing. Having a workable menu plan will usually make the difference between spending and saving.

After a number of years of experimenting with highly structured menu plans, I have settled contentedly into a relaxed approach for deciding what to make. At some point during the day in question— sometimes as late as fifteen minutes before a meal is served—I browse through my Recipe Roster options until I see something that fits my needs. If it has been a particularly busy day, I check the Fix-It-Fast Index. If nothing sounds appealing, I look under the Cooking in Quantity or Dry Mix sections for super-quick meal starts. If I am having company for dinner and the day is young, I check under Company's Coming. If there is leftover turkey meat, I look under Turkey.

The Recipe Roster eliminates the need for me to think of something off the top of my head, thereby reducing the mental stress of having to come up with fresh ideas day after day. The impromptu plan works because I have a stocked pantry with all the ingredients I need to make anything in my recipe repertoire.

If you feel better planning farther ahead, the thirty-day rotation system worked well for me for a long time. You could create a separate section for this, if you like, in your Kitchen Notebook, placing recipes for thirty-five of your favorite meals in one section. Or, you could simply create a thirty-five-grid chart that shows the names of the recipes to be served each day. With the chart method, you can keep your actual recipes in their separate notebook sections (Chinese, Mexican, Turkey, and so on).

The chart on page 140 illustrates what a month of meals at the Swedbergs might look like. It lists only entrées (but could include side dishes and desserts), features a few repetitive meals, and takes advantage of all my time- and money-saving principles. The schedule is flexible yet provides some structure, and keeps my pantry needs simple (I stock items for thirty-five recipes instead of an unlimited number of recipes).

I have introduced numerous food strategies so far in this book, and by walking through this menu plan together I can show you how it actually works.

You will notice that roast and steak appear often. We enjoy steak for supper on Saturday nights and I stock up when boneless chuck or pork steak goes on sale. Our favorite side dishes include Oven Hash Browns (page 98), corn (preferably on the cob), and Frosty Fruit Drinks (page 104).

Traditional Sunday fare is roast, potatoes, and carrots. It takes me a few minutes to get the roaster ready before church in the morning and about fifteen minutes to pull everything together once we get home. I usually bake a pan of refrigerator biscuits while the gravy thickens (quick gravy dry mix recipe on page 81). As the kids set the table I combine fruit cocktail, raisins, and whipped topping and scoop it into dessert dishes.

When making Chow Mein (page 123) for Monday's supper, I have three meat options: leftover roast beef, leftover turkey or chicken meat, or raw chicken breast (which I would have to dice and stir-fry before adding to the recipe). Chow mein includes the vegetables and meat; the obvious grain side dish is rice. Plain fruit works well with this meal. If you use ready-to-heat meals for lunches, make a larger than normal batch and divide individual portions into freezer containers. If you bury the rice under a layer of chow mein it will freeze, thaw, and reheat nicely.

Tuesday's Chicken in a Jiffy (page 29) is quick, easy, and impressive. I usually just scrub some potatoes, poke them with a fork, and put them in the oven at the same time I start the chicken. The mushrooms help to make dinner a bit special. A green vegetable such as broccoli and a colorful fresh fruit salad add variety. Refrigerator biscuits are a natural since oven temperatures match.

As a rule, a colorful meal is both appetizing and nutritious. The above meal would suffice with chicken, potatoes, gravy, cauliflower, and a banana-nut salad, but it might not please the eye. If you aren't in the habit of color-coordinating your meals, consider starting sections in your Recipe Roster for Side Dishes: Green, Side Dishes: Red, and so on. Soon you'll automatically select foods that draw compliments even before they've been tasted.

Wednesday's meal may take about ten minutes or two hours of work. It depends on whether ground beef went on sale recently. If I stocked up this week, tonight would be my chance to do something with all that bargain meat. Taking advantage of quantity cooking principles, I would make a big batch of meat loaf (Seasoning Mix recipe on page 90) and put one in the oven for our supper as quickly as possible. As soon as supper's entrée, the meat loaf, was baking I would assemble the other meat loaves (in this example, two more) and start browning some of the remaining ground beef on the range. I would brown the meat on low heat so I wouldn't have to stand over it. If you like to sauté your meat with onions and green pepper, allow extra time for chopping.

While the meat was browning, I would assemble a big batch of meatballs (using the Meat Loaf Seasoning Mix for these as well) and place them very close together, but not touching, on cookie sheets. As soon as a sheet was full, I would slide it into the freezer, stir the browning meat, and fill the next tray. When the meatballs were done, I would start a pan of water boiling for the egg noodles that we will enjoy with tonight's meat loaf.

Working quickly, I would shape the remaining ground beef into patties. I like to add Spike seasoning, oatmeal, and an egg to the meat before forming the patties. I would place the individual burgers in heavy-duty plastic wrap and then place enough for one meal in a zip-top bag. Once I finished, I would add the noodles to the water and set the table. I would shred some lettuce into a bowl and add a drained can of mandarin oranges, a few slivered almonds, and a drizzle of honey. Getting everyone to the table would take the last few minutes of noodle prep-time.

After supper I would drain the fat off the browned meat and measure out 2 cups per freezer-quality zip-top bag, label, and freeze. Before bed I would transfer the frozen meatballs into a clean, empty, 5-quart ice cream bucket and put it in the freezer.

The hour before dinner was *very* busy, but I am now the proud owner of a freezer full of ground-beef-meal starts. Think of the time savings (and money savings since the meat was at its lowest price). The next eight times I need browned beef I won't need to take out a pan, crumble the meat, stand over the range stirring, drain the grease, wash the pan, or put it away. I will simply grab a bag, crack it on the counter to break up the pieces, and dump it into my casserole.

The next four times I need meatballs, there will be no mess and no fuss. I will just count out how many I want, reseal the bucket, and voilà! I also have four hamburger meals and two more meat loaves. I was going to make the meat loaf mess anyway, and look what my hour produced. Over a period of months, how many hours do you spend on all these unnecessary steps?

Onward! So I don't lose you completely, sing the next few lines to the tune "Home, Home on the Range":

> Oh is there a home, where the pizza fans roam
> Where the mother and father are broke?
> Where never is heard, an encouraging word
> Unless pizza is served every day?
> Home, in the U.S.
> Where the pizza shops rake in the bucks;
> This dish is a cinch,
> A great hit in a pinch,
> And everyone's happy all day.

My busy sister-in-law with five hollow-legged boys ages seven to twenty tipped me off to Poppin' Pizzas (page 34). If it fills up her crew, it might work for you, too. Once again, Frosty Fruit Drinks (page 104) are the only standard pizza accompaniment for my family.

Turkey Meatballs Tetrazzini (page 31) is a fancy name for a range-top noodle casserole. This all-in-one dish leaves out only the fruit. It is a great meal to expand, but freeze it after cooking. To ensure that noodles taste the best when reheated, slightly undercook the portion you plan to freeze.

Jump to Monday's turkey. You may have been wondering how I come up with leftover turkey. Here's the spot. Once or twice a month I make a Thanksgiving-size turkey or large turkey breast. Occasionally I make stuffing (recipe on page 54) and use the extras for an expanded recipe of Layered Turkey Bake (page 47), but more often I just bake potatoes. I always make gravy and use the pan juices for stew. You could pay several dollars per pound for deli turkey meat or you could buy large birds for a fraction of that cost and earn the difference quite easily. Freeze meat in meal-size portions.

If your family insists on the "see whole turkey, eat whole turkey" mentality, consider cooking your bird overnight at 250°F. This gives you the opportunity to take care of the turkey in the morning, after it has cooked and cooled, and when your family will not be so tempted to devour a Thanksgiving-size meal. You may be able to stash all the meat before they know you've even cooked a bird.

If that seems like stealing food from your precious offspring or spouse, consider this comparison. Have you ever bought a package of Double Stuffed Oreos and hid them so they wouldn't be devoured before nightfall? The turkey strategy is not much different and probably for a better cause. The amount of turkey meat required in a casserole dinner for four is equal to only a pound or so of meat, while the amount you consume when you serve turkey as the main course is closer to a pound per person.

Tuesday's Yorkshire Strata (page 28) is a fancy dinner that goes together quickly, especially if you use leftover meat and vegetables. But beware, it will fall fast! Serve an appetizer soup or salad during the final few minutes of cooking time and then introduce the main course directly from oven to table. A fruit of any kind can serve as dessert.

Wednesday we can use either meatballs or browned beef for our spaghetti. Start the meat and noodles at the same time, assemble the sauce, and make a lettuce salad. Butter some bread and cut it into 1-inch strips (I use a kitchen scissor for this). Place strips on a greased cookie sheet, sprinkle with garlic salt, and broil for about 3 minutes (watch carefully). Serve in a napkin-lined wicker basket.

Stir-fry is much the same routine as Chow Mein. Oven-Fried Chicken follows the same recipe as Chicken in a Jiffy (page 29), except I serve sour cream on the potatoes instead of gravy.

Monday night's Turkey Rice Pilaf (page 30) utilizes leftover turkey meat and is accompanied by peach halves atop a lettuce bed. Tuesday's Tacos require a bit of dicing, but leftover salad fixings are great with the upcoming Meatballs Consommé. Instead of pricey and fragile taco shells, I use the inexpensive El DeliGran Nacho Chips. Each person makes a bed of chips, crushes them slightly, and then layers on their favorite taco ingredients.

Sweet 'N' Sour Chicken uses the inexpensive chicken leg quarters, which I bake with a coating of Sweet 'N' Sour Sauce (page 125) in a 350°F oven for 70 minutes. A green vegetable served atop angel hair noodles (which cook quickly) with Parmesan cheese makes a pretty side dish. Broiled garlic bread and a fruit salad featuring pineapple make this mealtime memorable.

Meatballs Consommé (page 35) over mashed potatoes is a favorite from my childhood. A lettuce salad using the leftover taco ingredients and a plain fruit dessert accent this classic meat-and-potatoes meal. The next new meal comes four days later: BBQ Meatballs (meatballs with a coating of the first barbecue sauce recipe on page 130). I usually serve this with Oven Hash Browns (page 98) using leftover potatoes from Sunday's lunch. Peas and Frosty Fruit Cups (page 55) round off this great dinner.

When I make Layered Tamale Pie (page 45), I make four. These freeze nicely and are always welcome meals to send to a family in need. Add a fruit salad with mini-marshmallows and whipped topping plus a side of corn bread.

Ham and potatoes is a breeze. I use the dinner slices the butcher cut for me when turkey ham was on sale. I place overlapping ham slices on the bottom of a casserole dish, pour on some Ham Glaze (page 131), cover tightly with aluminum foil, and bake for 45 minutes at 325°F. I scrub some potatoes and slide them into the oven at the same time. Served with sour cream, a vegetable of any kind (or color), buns, and a fruit cocktail and banana salad, this dinner is a taste treat.

Turkey Salsa Quickies (page 27) can be garnished with lots of shredded lettuce and tomatoes. Served with raw broccoli and orange slices, this makes an easy, balanced meal.

That completes the rotation. You may be wondering what I do with the rest of the hamburger, turkey meat, and so on. I have the privilege of serving my family of five three meals per day, everyday of the week, all year long. My husband works close enough to home to join us during his lunch hour and my three children are home-schooled, so they also enjoy all twenty-one meals each week at our table. And as I have already mentioned, we entertain a great deal, so using up those extra entrées is never a problem.

If your lunches are provided for economically by an outside source, or if you have a smaller family, making big batches as frequently as I do would not be prudent. If your family is twice the size of mine, however, you may find yourself making even bigger batches on a more frequent basis. Remember, all the recipes leave room for you to write in your quantity adjustments.

You've seen how I plugged in my traditional meals; your menu plan should reflect your favorites. Some of my friends have pizza every Friday night and others use a system of theme variations: Mondays may feature Italian, Tuesdays chicken, Wednesdays a breakfast-type meal, and so on. Personalize your plan by choosing foods that you enjoy, and make it practical by selecting meals that are easy to assemble. Be sure to include some entrées that can be expanded and also take advantage of dry mixes as often as possible.

Once your plan is written out, make numerous copies. Post one on your kitchen bulletin board and file the others in your Kitchen Notebook. If your scheduled meal won't work, simply replace it with a fast fix or previously expanded freezer meal. Either forget the planned meal altogether or use it instead of an upcoming, more time-consuming entrée. The goal of a menu plan is freedom and flexibility. It is not supposed to box you in or limit you in any way.

MENU ROTATION PLAN

Sunday	Monday	Tuesday	Wednesday	Thursday	Friday	Saturday
Roast	Chow Mein	Chicken in a Jiffy	Meatloaf	Poppin' Pizza	Turkey Meatballs Tetrazzini	Steak
Roast	Turkey	Yorkshire Strata	Spaghetti	Stir-Fry	Oven-Fried Chicken	Steak
Roast	Turkey Rice Pilaf	Tacos	Sweet 'N' Sour Chicken	Meatballs Consommé	Chow Mein	Steak
Roast	BBQ Meatballs	Stir-Fry	Layered Tamale Pie	Layered Turkey Bake	Deep-Dish Pizza	Steak
Roast	Ham and Potatoes	Spaghetti Pie	Stir-Fry	Turkey Salsa Quickies	Pizza Roll-Ups	Steak

10.

Bread and Chocolate: Homemade Favorites for Family and Friends

Most of the recipes in this chapter are excellent for gifts, and most, at first glance, will seem expensive in one or more ways. Fudge, for example, contains costly ingredients and is outrageously fattening. However, the county fair winning recipe on page 145 tastes at least as good as the candy store variety for a fraction of the cost per pound. When you want to give someone a gift from your heart, sweets like fudge and the ice cream toppings on page 146–147 can't be beat.

People appreciate the significance of homemade gifts because of the time invested and the love poured into them. But fresh and familiar ingredients make home-baked goodness especially welcome. According to the FDA Superintendent of Documents, mass-produced baked breads are allowed to contain up to 125 ingredients while listing only 8 on the bag. The logic seems to be that the 100 or more other ingredients are "normal and standard" additives. The recipes in this section call for 6 to 12 ingredients, so I don't see how more than 100 could be considered insignificant enough to escape the bagged bread's list!

If you want to provide your family with nutritious baked goods or offer your friends the best of the best, the following baking tips will be invaluable.

Bakery Tips

1. I used to wonder why bread recipes gave such a large range of flour measurements. To a novice baker the responsibility of deciding whether to add the minimum 6 cups or the maximum 8 cups can be intimidating. If you are unsure how much to add during the second stage of mixing, stop adding when the dough pulls away easily from the sides of the bowl. Another tip at this stage is to add the flour gradually—about a cup at a time. This allows it to work into the original dough before more is added.

2. Before the first rising, grease the bowl with margarine on a paper towel. Once the dough is in the bowl, turn it over a few times to coat the exterior with the oil.

3. If you are not confident that the bread is fully baked at the end of the baking period, remove it from the pan and tap the bottom. It will give you a hollow sound if the center is done. If the top of the bread is getting too brown before the bread is fully baked, lay a piece of aluminum foil loosely over the bread.

4. To achieve the greatest cost savings when baking, buy yeast at a co-op for a mere 7 percent (!) of the individual grocery store packet price.

Flour Power

There are so many varieties of flour on the market that it is important for you to realize that some react differently from others. The following tips can save you time, money, and a lot of frustration.

1. Always use the amount and type of flour called for in any given recipe unless you are willing to risk a product that varies slightly from the creator's intent.

2. Whole wheat flour may be substituted for white flour in most recipes up to 50 percent; in other words, 1 cup all-purpose flour may be replaced with ½ cup all-purpose flour plus ½ cup whole wheat flour.

3. White and whole wheat flour contain a protein called gluten, which gives them their unique baking ability. Most other flours do not have gluten, either in the same quantity or at all. They offer less satisfactory bread-baking results. If you wish to use another type of flour, substitute only ⅛ cup per cup of regular flour. An example would be 1 cup all-purpose flour replaced with ⅞ cup all-purpose flour plus ⅛ cup potato flour.

If making bread from scratch is not a possibility for you, consider buying frozen bread dough when it goes on sale. You get the smell of fresh-baked homemade bread without any mess or fuss, and the dough costs about a quarter the price of ready-made loaves. One caution about frozen bread dough: You must use it within thirty days or it may not rise properly. One solution is to bake all the loaves and freeze some for later.

If you have no time at all for baking, try shopping at a bakery thrift store for day-old bread. Believe me, with more than a hundred mold inhibitors and shape enhancers, the bread is perfectly fine after twenty-four hours! In fact, one of the biggest surprises with home-baked bread is the speed with which it gets moldy, sometimes within five days if kept at room temperature. If you are baking bread from scratch or from frozen bread dough, be sure to freeze all portions that will not be consumed within a few days, and then thaw additional loaves as needed.

Snacks to Pack

If you do not thrill to the idea of becoming a baker, maybe one of the snacks on pages 156–161 will spark your interest. Hikers enjoy the taste of store-bought Trail Mix, but it can add up to big bucks in a hurry. Make your own personalized mix by combining equal parts of your favorite sale-priced ingredients. Suggestions include raisins, almonds, pecans, walnuts, peanuts, sunflower seeds, dried fruit, chocolate/carob chips, M&M's, or anything else you enjoy. Once again, a food co-op would offer significant price savings on nuts, dried fruits, and carob chips. Stir well and pour into pint-size zip-tops. These compact pouches keep indefinitely.

Sixteen Recipes for Breads, Sweets,
and Packable Snacks

Sweetened Condensed Milk

As a baking ingredient, Sweetened Condensed Milk is used frequently
in candy and dessert recipes. This homemade version costs about
one-fifth what you'd pay in a store. The original version can be substituted in any recipe; the fat-free version offers a slightly different
consistency, but works in most recipes.

Ingredients	Quantity for original version	Quantity for fat-free version
Sugar	⅓ cup	¾ cup
Nonfat dry milk powder	1 cup	1 cup plus 2 tablespoons
Boiling water	⅓ cup	½ cup
Margarine, melted	3 tablespoons	
Yield (equivalent)	1 can, for a total of @963 calories/26 grams fat	1 can, for a total of @806 calories/4 grams fat

Combine all ingredients in blender container and whir on high until
smooth. Keeps well in the refrigerator indefinitely.

Candy Store Fudge

Ingredients	Quantity	_X Quantity
Sugar	2¼ cups	
Evaporated milk	6 ounces	
Chocolate chips	18 ounces	
Marshmallow cream	4 ounces	
Margarine	¼ pound	
Chopped nuts	2 cups	
Yield	1 9 by 9-inch pan	

Bring sugar and milk to a boil over medium-high heat; reduce heat and simmer, stirring constantly, for 9 minutes. All at once, add the chips, cream, and margarine; stir until melted. Stir in nuts, spread into a lightly greased pan, and chill. Cut and serve.

Caramel Sauce

This excellent sauce goes together quickly in the microwave.

Ingredients	Quantity	Quantity for fat-free version
Margarine, melted	4 tablespoons	
Corn syrup	2 tablespoons	⅓ cup
Brown sugar	1 cup	½ cup
Milk or cream	⅓ cup	
Liquid nonfat milk		4 tablespoons
Cornstarch		1 teaspoon
Vanilla	1 teaspoon	1 teaspoon
Yield	1½ cups	⅔ cup

Instructions for Original Version

Blend together margarine, corn syrup, brown sugar, and milk. Microwave on high for 3 to 4 minutes, stirring after each 60-second interval. Add vanilla and stir to blend. Serve warm or cold.

Instructions for Fat-Free Version

Microwave corn syrup, brown sugar, and 3 tablespoons of the liquid nonfat milk on high until boiling. Stir and microwave on high for 1 minute longer. Combine the remaining tablespoon of nonfat milk with 1 teaspoon cornstarch and stir to blend. Stirring the heated mixture constantly, gradually add the cornstarch combination. Microwave on high for 30 seconds longer; stir. Add vanilla and serve warm or cold.

Chocolate Syrup

This truly excellent syrup can be made for less than a fourth the cost of the commercial brands.

Ingredients	Quantity	Quantity for fat-free version
Liquid nonfat milk		1 cup
Milk	1 cup	
Margarine	1 tablespoon	
White sugar	2 cups	2 cups
Unsweetened cocoa powder	½ cup	½ cup
Vanilla	½ teaspoon	½ teaspoon
Yield	2 cups, for a total of 1,940 calories/22 grams fat	2 cups, for a total of 1,790 calories/ 4 grams fat

Combine all ingredients in a blender and whir for a few seconds until cocoa powder is blended. Heat over medium heat on stove top or in microwave on high, stirring often, until hot. Do not boil. Serve hot or cold over ice cream, or add a tablespoon to a glass of cold or hot milk for chocolate milk or hot cocoa.

Maple Syrup

Perfect for your family or as a holiday hostess gift. Create your own maple syrup on the stove top while you make the pancakes and both will be ready at the same time. At one-fourth the price of the leading brand, this syrup can't be beat!

Ingredients	Quantity	_X Quantity
Brown sugar	2 cups	
Sugar	1 cup	
Water	1 ⅓ cups	
Maple extract	2 teaspoons	
Yield	2 ⅔ cups	

Combine the sugars and water in a saucepan over medium-high heat; bring to a boil. Remove from heat and add extract. Pour into a clean jar and refrigerate indefinitely.

Note: This syrup tastes great immediately, but it will get substantially thicker after being in the refrigerator for a few hours.

Frostings

Your special baked goods will shine with these easy, inexpensive, and delightful frostings. They can be made for roughly a quarter of the price of canned frosting and they taste better and have fewer preservatives, too.

Ingredients	Quantity for white frosting	Quantity for chocolate frosting
Powdered sugar	3 cups	3 cups
Shortening	½ cup	½ cup
Cocoa	—	¾ cup
Hot tap water	4 teaspoons	3 tablespoons
Extract of choice	1 teaspoon	1 teaspoon
Yield	1½ cups	1½ cups

For chocolate frosting, stir together the sugar and cocoa until well blended, then proceed as follows. Cream the sugar and shortening, adding water as needed until of spreadable consistency. Add the extract as follows:

Vanilla: 1 teaspoon

Peppermint: 1 teaspoon plus a few drops of green food coloring

Almond: 1 teaspoon, and then sprinkle finished dessert with slivered or sliced almonds

Maple: 1 teaspoon

Other Frosting Flavors:

Mocha: Add ½ tablespoon fine instant coffee granules to chocolate frosting; mix well.

Lemon: Replace the water with lemon juice, and omit the extract.

Orange: Add 2 egg yolks and 1 teaspoon grated orange peel, and reduce the water to 2 tablespoons.

Peanut butter: Replace the shortening in the white frosting recipe with peanut butter and increase the water to ½ cup.

Honey Wheat Bread

If you usually buy wheat bread at the store, you will appreciate the excellent flavor of this particularly easy recipe.

Ingredient	Quantity	4X Quantity	_X Quantity
Yeast	1 tablespoon	4 tablespoons	
Warm water	¾ cup	1 cup	
Sugar	1 teaspoon	2 teaspoons	
Whole wheat flour	¾ cup	3 cups	
All-purpose flour	2 cups	8 cups	
Salt	1 teaspoon	2 teaspoons	
Water		2 cups	
Eggs	1	4	
Honey	3 tablespoons	¾ cup	
Margarine	2 tablespoons	¼ pound	
Yield	1 loaf	4 loaves	

Combine yeast, warm water, and sugar; set aside. Combine flours and salt; add remaining ingredients, including yeast combination, and stir until well blended. Knead for 10 minutes, adding additional all-purpose flour as needed. Let rise in a greased bowl until doubled in bulk (about 1 hour). Form loaf, place in a greased loaf pan, and let rise for 45 minutes longer. Bake at 375°F for 25 to 30 minutes. Cool on rack.

Crescent Rolls

Dress up any meal with these delicious rolls.

Ingredients	Quantity	_X Quantity
Yeast	1 tablespoon	
Warm water	1 cup	
Sugar	1 teaspoon	
Evaporated milk	¾ cup	
Sugar	⅓ cup	
Salt	1½ teaspoons	
Egg	1	
Flour	1½ cups	
Oil	¼ cup	
Flour	4 cups	
Margarine, cold	½ pound	
Yield	32 small rolls	

Activate yeast in warm water and sugar; set aside. In a small mixing bowl, combine milk, sugar, salt, egg, and 1½ cups flour. Beat to a smooth batter, add the yeast, blend well, and finally add the oil, stirring until smooth.

In a large mixing bowl, cut margarine into the 4 cups flour until about the size of kidney beans. (I do all of this with my electric mixer, changing at this point to dough hooks.) Pour yeast batter over all and blend until smooth. Cover and refrigerate for at least 4 hours. If you can't get back to it, this dough keeps well in the refrigerator for up to 4 days.

When ready to proceed, knead the dough a few times to remove air pockets, then divide into four equal parts. Place three parts back in the refrigerator, and roll out the fourth into a 12-inch circle on a lightly floured surface. Cut 8 equal pie shapes (or 6 for sandwich-size buns). Roll toward the point and shape into crescents on ungreased baking sheets. Repeat with all dough and let rise for 4 hours. Bake at 325°F for 18 minutes, or until golden brown. Cool on racks.

Brown 'N' Serve Option

Prepare dough as directed except bake at 300°F for only 12 minutes (until firm but not cooked through). Cool on racks and store in refrigerator for up to 2 days or freeze for up to 3 months.

To bake: Place frozen or chilled buns on an ungreased baking sheet and bake in preheated 400°F oven for about 10 minutes, until golden.

Filled Crescents

Before rolling crescents, spread jam or cream cheese on rolled-out dough. Roll up and proceed as directed.

Note of interest: This dough may be used anytime crescent roll dough or puff pastry is called for in any of your favorite recipes.

French Croissants

This recipe is simple enough for novices and costs just pennies per roll.

Ingredients	Quantity	_X Quantity
Flour	⅓ cup	
Margarine	¾ pound	
Yeast	2 tablespoons	
Warm water	½ cup	
Sugar	¼ cup plus 1 teaspoon	
Milk	¾ cup	
Salt	1 teaspoon	
Egg	1	
Flour	4½ cups	
Yield	32 croissants	

Cream ⅓ cup flour and margarine; roll between wax paper to a 6 by 12-inch rectangle. Chill for at least 1 hour.

Combine yeast, warm water, and 1 teaspoon sugar; set aside. Scald milk, ¼ cup sugar, and salt in microwave on high for 2 minutes. Stir. Let cool to lukewarm, then add the egg and the yeast mixture. Beat until smooth. Mix in 2 cups flour, then proceed by hand, or switch to a dough hook, if available.

Blend in enough of the remaining flour to make a soft dough; knead for 7 to 10 minutes, or until it feels soft and elastic.

The next part of the recipe is what makes croissants unique. Be careful to use very little additional flour and to rechill the dough as needed.

Roll out the dough into a 14-inch square on a lightly floured surface. Place the chilled margarine mixture onto the dough, covering half the surface. Bring other half over, like a blanket, and seal edges. Roll out to a 12 by 21-inch rectangle; fold in thirds. Continue rolling out and folding into thirds until you have done it three times. If margarine becomes too soft, chill dough for 15 minutes, then continue. Place in plastic wrap and chill for 45 minutes.

Cut chilled dough into four equal parts, returning three to refrigerator. Roll out the fourth to a 10-inch circle; cut into 8 pie-shaped wedges. Roll toward the point and curve gently into a crescent shape. Place on ungreased baking sheet. Repeat until all four sections are formed. Let rise until doubled in bulk (about 45 minutes). Brush on a little milk and egg yolk, if desired, and bake at 375°F for 12 to 15 minutes, until golden. Cool on racks.

Variations:

Before cutting croissants from the 10-inch circle, spread a favorite filling over the surface; cut, roll, and proceed as directed. My favorite fillings are cream cheese and chocolate frosting.

French or Italian Loaves

These loaves are always in great demand for cheese bread and hot hoagies.

Ingredients	Quantity	_X Quantity
Milk	½ cup	
Water	1 cup	
Oil	¼ cup	
Sugar	1 tablespoon plus 2 teaspoons	
Yeast	1 tablespoon	
Warm water	¼ cup	
Flour	4 cups	
Salt	2 teaspoons	
Yield (French bread)	2 24-inch loaves	
(Italian bread)	3 11-inch loaves	

Microwave milk on high for 1 minute; set aside. Combine water, oil, and 1 tablespoon sugar; set aside. Mix together the yeast, 2 teaspoons sugar and warm water; set aside. Measure flour and salt into a large mixing bowl. Stir to distribute salt, then add all the previously combined ingredients, stirring until well blended. Knead on a floured surface until smooth, about 8 minutes.

Let dough rest in mixing bowl for 2 hours. Form loaves as desired and place on greased baking sheets. Cut diagonal, ¼-inch-deep slashes on the top of the dough. Let rise for 45 minutes. Bake at 400°F for 15 minutes, reduce heat to 350°F, and bake for an additional 30 minutes, placing a piece of aluminum foil over the top for the last 30 minutes.

Cool loaves on racks and freeze any you will not use within 3 days.

Sugar and Spice Nuts

In a decorative container, this mix makes an excellent hostess gift.

Ingredients	Quantity	_X Quantity
Water	2 tablespoons	
Egg	1	
Sugar	½ cup	
Salt	½ teaspoon	
Cinnamon	¼ teaspoon	
Allspice	¼ teaspoon	
Pumpkin pie seasoning	¼ teaspoon	
Nuts of choice	2 cups	
Yield	2 cups	

Mix all ingredients, adding nuts after the other ingredients have been stirred. Spread mixture on an ungreased cookie sheet and bake at 250°F for 1 hour, stirring every 15 minutes.

Poppycock

Caramel corn never tasted so good!

Ingredients	Quantity	_X Quantity
Popcorn	½ cup	
Mixed nuts	2 cups	
Brown sugar	¾ cup	
Margarine	6 tablespoons	
Corn syrup	3 tablespoons	
Salt	½ teaspoon	
Baking soda	½ teaspoon	
Yield	3 quarts	

Pop the corn and place it in a large paper grocery bag with the mixed nuts. Combine sugar, margarine, corn syrup, and salt; microwave on high for 4 minutes, stirring after each minute. Stir in the baking soda and pour this mixture immediately over the popped corn in the bag. Shake vigorously for 45 seconds; place bag in microwave and cook on high for 3 minutes. Shake vigorously. Serve immediately or store in moistureproof, airtight containers at room temperature for up to 1 month.

Granola

Delicious as a cereal or snack.

Ingredients	Quantity	_X Quantity
Brown sugar	1 cup	
Cinnamon	1 tablespoon	
Salt	1 teaspoon	
Oil	½ cup	
Water	¼ cup	
Vanilla	2 teaspoons	
Quick oats	6 cups	
Nuts and sunflower seeds	2 cups	
Coconut	1 cup	
Wheat germ	1 cup	
Yield	11 cups	

Combine the sugar, cinnamon, salt, oil, water, and vanilla; set aside. Mix together the remaining ingredients. Combine all ingredients and stir until coated. Spread on two greased cookie sheets; bake at 350°F for 30 minutes, until golden. Watch so it does not get too dark. Store completely cooled granola in a moistureproof, airtight container at room temperature for up to 6 months.

Mounds Bars

Everyone will be after you for this recipe.

Ingredients	Quantity	_X Quantity
Mashed potatoes	¾ cup	
Coconut	4 cups	
Powdered sugar	4 cups	
Vanilla	1 teaspoon	
Chocolate chips	12 ounces	
Yield	50 bars or 1 8 by 8-inch pan	

Combine the potatoes, coconut, sugar, and vanilla. If making pan bars, sprinkle more powdered sugar over the bottom of your pan and spread in filling, pressing until evenly distributed. If making individual bars, form the size of bars you desire and place on a cooling rack. Refrigerate for 1 hour. Melt chocolate chips and either frost the pan bars or dip the individual bars into the chocolate, allowing excess to drip off before returning them to cooling racks to harden. Return bars to refrigerator until needed.

Peanut Butter Cups

Traditionally a holiday treat, these easy candies offer terrific savings over the prepackaged variety.

Ingredients	Quantity	_X Quantity
Powdered sugar	2 cups	
Peanut butter	1½ cups	
Margarine, room temperature	3 tablespoons	
Chocolate bark	12 ounces	
Yield	100 cups	

Mix together sugar, peanut butter, and margarine; form into ½-inch balls and flatten a bit on a baking sheet. Chill until firm. Melt the bark and dip the bottom of each ball into it. Place balls into individual miniature muffin-cup liners or candy liners. Pour chocolate over top in a slow drizzle to coat. Let set until firm. Store in airtight containers at room temperature for up to 1 month or in the freezer for up to 6 months.

Tootsie Rolls

My kids love to make these excellent look-alike candies.

Ingredients	Quantity	_X Quantity
Unsweetened chocolate	1 square	
Butter	1 tablespoon	
Corn syrup	¼ cup	
Vanilla	¼ teaspoon	
Nonfat dry milk powder	⅓ cup	
Powdered sugar	1+ cup	
Yield	30 tootsie rolls	

Melt chocolate and butter together; stir in corn syrup and vanilla and mix well. Add milk powder. Measure sugar onto the counter and knead chocolate combination into it until it does not stick anymore. This may require up to 1½ cups powdered sugar. Divide and roll in long, pencil-thin strips; cut with a knife into 1-inch sections. Store rolls in an airtight container in the refrigerator until needed.

11.

Lean and Luscious

After an entire chapter of fattening foods it seems only fitting to write a chapter about dieting, right? For most of my life I have been self-conscious about my figure, and I have made a nearly full-time job for myself out of hunting for the best diet and exercise programs. Only in the past few years have I found foods that are both low in fat and satisfying. While my education in the "School of Hard Knocks" gives me the courage to offer tips for reducing fat in your diet, I am not in any other way qualified to address nutritional interests. Please consult your physician before beginning any new dietary regimen.

There are three books that I can wholeheartedly recommend when it comes to weight control. While the titles may seem contradictory, the messages of each are helpful in their own way.

The Underburner's Diet, by Dr. Barbara Edelstein (NY: Macmillan Publishing Co., 1987), is my favorite. Her tongue-in-cheek approach to the realities of life for folks not blessed with high-speed metabolisms helped me make more reasonable goals and achieve them. *Telling Yourself the Truth*, by William Backus and Marie Chapian (Hampshire, MN: Bethany House Publications, 1980), is not strictly a diet book but addresses some of the underlying reasons we can feel overwhelmed in this ongoing battle. Finally, *Diets Don't Work*, by Bob Schwartz (Houston, TX: Breakthru Publishing, 1982), helped me to identify some "leaks" in my psychological approach to food. His great advice to "disconnect the eating machine" and enjoy every bite makes a lot of sense.

The food intake section of your Kitchen Notebook provides a

place to write down every bite you eat, thereby minimizing senseless eating behaviors. Simply knowing that you will have to record those five chocolate chip cookies at 285 calories and 16.5 grams of fat may inspire you to "binge" on five Kiss Delights (page 169) instead. You would save 240 calories and every last one of those fat grams!

Expansion cooking techniques offer hefty financial advantages for diet dinner fans. If you have ever enjoyed the freedom of portioned and assembled convenience dinners, you may also have lamented the fact that food manufacturers are selling these little treasures at huge markups. Between the substitution suggestions later in this chapter and the many options listed in the Substitutions and Equivalents guide (page 178) you can defat many of your favorite recipes and make expanded, ready-to-heat frozen diet dinners that will provide variety and financial savings.

Tips on Reading Labels

Since too many little fat grams add up to big hips, be on the lookout for new fat-free or low-fat products and try to use the lowest-fat version that you can find. Beware of labeling intended to deceive: Always check the label to find out exactly how many calories are from fat. Legal requirements ensure that accurate and understandable information is shown in the boxed nutrition panel, but some food labels are still confusing. Instead of honestly exposing the percentage of fat content by calorie, some food manufacturers use labels that indicate the percent of fat by grams—comparing the total grams of food to the total grams (not calories) of fat. Since each fat gram equals nine calories, something that claims to be 94 percent fat free could actually be made of up to 70 percent fat. Sounds odd, but it's true.

If you are uncertain of current diet lingo, here is a quick reference guide to assist you in your efforts to make wise decisions:

Calorie free: less than 5 calories per serving

Sugar free: less than .5 grams sugar per serving

Salt free: less than 5 milligrams sodium per serving

Fat free: less than .5 grams fat per serving (providing it has no added fat or oil ingredients)

Low fat: less than 3 grams fat per serving or per 100 grams of food

Light: contains one-third fewer calories than its original product

Substitution Guidelines

Use the following substitutes to create lower-in-fat versions of your otherwise high-fat recipes.

Cooking oils. Your daily fat intake should not exceed 30 percent of your total diet, and saturated fats should be kept to a minimum. It is the saturated fats that have the most negative impact on blood cholesterol. When oil is required in a recipe, I choose canola oil because it contains fewer than 6.4 grams of saturated fat per 100 grams. Other good options include corn, safflower, and olive oil, which all contain fewer than 12 grams of saturated fat per 100 grams. Try to avoid the use of peanut oil and margarine, each boasting 18 to 19 grams, cottonseed oil at 25 grams, and butter at a whopping 46 grams of saturated fat per 100 grams. Remember that all oils are 100 percent fat, and that the difference lies only in the percentage of saturated fat that each one contains.

Substituting fats. Whenever feasible, replace oil, shortening, and margarine with a low-fat or nonfat alternative. Applesauce and yogurt, the usually recommended fat substitutes, yield mostly tough and unsatisfactory results. My favorite substitute is evaporated skim milk, which if used cup for cup instead of oil or shortening gives the richest taste for the least fat grams. Save money by making your own (page 202). Another substitute that works well is reconstituted buttermilk powder. Do not use buttermilk purchased from the dairy case because this is high in fat. Buttermilk powder is usually available in the baking section of the grocery store or from food clubs. Finally, for baking situations, the suggestions in Oil and Sugar Substitutes (page 206) work well.

Salad dressings. Miracle Whip Free is a boon to the fat-conscious eater. Consider that real mayonnaise contains up to 14 grams of fat per tablespoon, commercial salad dressings about 10 grams of fat, and Miracle Whip Free *none*. When substituting fat-free salad dressing in recipes calling for its high-fat alternative, a liquid adjustment may be required: Fat-free tends to be more dense. I usually assemble the recipe as directed, substituting wherever possible, and then add liquid fat-free milk until I achieve the desired consistency.

Nonfat milk. I rely completely on liquid nonfat milk and non-fat dry milk powder for personal use. Powdered milk costs far less than milk in any other form and works well for use in dry mixes and most recipes, with the exception of pudding. Liquid nonfat milk, available in most dairy cases, is sometimes more expensive than whole milk but offers a savings of 50 calories and 8.6 fat grams per cup.

Eggs. The fat in eggs is found in the yolk; the white contains only 16 of an egg's 70 or so calories and none of its 7 grams of fat. In most cooking and baking situations, you can substitute 2 egg whites for each egg called for. For example, if the recipe calls for 3 eggs, use 6 egg whites and throw away the yolks. If you can't bear to throw out yolks, try substituting 1 heaping teaspoon of soy flour plus 1 table-spoon water for each egg. This works for most baking situations. Soy flour is available through food co-ops and in most health-food stores.

Cheese. I am one of those people who think everything tastes better with cheese, so fat-free cheese options are a real blessing. Check your dairy case for possibilities or use the "defatting" tech-nique outlined on page 170, and then plan burritos for dinner.

Sour cream. Many recipes call for sour cream, and a recent ad-dition to the dairy case is a nonfat version offering a savings of 2.5 fat grams per tablespoon. My practice is to substitute the nonfat sour cream in all my recipes, but to go ahead and enjoy the taste and tex-ture of the real thing when it comes to topping my potato or taco. Ex-periment to decide what works for you: The nonfat option may meet your taste standards for every eating occasion.

Low-fat/low-sodium broth. Whenever you boil chicken or turkey, reserve the liquid for broth (for soups, in recipes calling for canned broth, etc.). When chilled, the fat rises to the top and can be easily spooned off. The remaining liquid makes a flavorful low-fat/low-sodium broth that can be frozen in ice cube trays or any other size container until needed.

Turkey meat. Most ground turkey burger contains around 28 fat grams per pound. If you own a meat grinder, you can create turkey burger with only 4.8 grams fat per pound by grinding up your skinless, boneless, cooked white turkey meat.

Making less seem like more. One trick that works great is to place fattening ingredients on top of your food instead of inside. Your eye somehow tricks your taste buds into enjoying more flavor than would seem logical. Do not hide the high-fat sausage under other ingredients on your pizza, but save it for last and spread approximately one-third your normal amount on top. When baking cookies, sprinkle a few chocolate chips atop each instead of mixing in the entire bag. You will use less than half the bag and enjoy a terrifically satisfying treat.

Mini-magic. Replacing regular chocolate chips with mini-morsels saves half the chips and gives the impression of chocolate. This works especially well in cakes and muffins.

Another chocolate tip. Whenever feasible, I replace chocolate squares or baking chips with unsweetened cocoa powder, which contains little fat. See the entries under "Chocolate" in the Substitutions and Equivalents guide on page 189. These options cost less money and contain fewer fat grams. Remember, baking squares and chocolate chips contain a bonding agent, often lecithin, that is required in some recipes. Do not attempt to substitute powder in mousse or foods that require hardening, such as candy.

Fat-Fighting Tips

As I mentioned earlier, my only qualifications for sharing tips with you regarding dieting is a history in the health club industry and my own day-to-day experience and observations. I have won at losing pounds numerous times, but the war will never be over for me. Fat molecules seem to enjoy congregating on my hips, and I rebel against their convention plans! My personal "battle of the bulge" is more successful when I abide by the following guidelines. I hope they will be of use to you also.

  1. Anything is okay in moderation. If you crave a certain food, have a little, eat it slowly and enjoy every bite, then stop. Eating too much ensures that you feel stuffed and out of control. Depriving yourself completely may set you up for the big binge later. Moderation is the key.

2. Eat only when you are truly hungry. Thin people have the self-confidence to say, "No, thank you. I'm just not hungry right now." Dieters hate saying this because they think it draws attention to their situation. So just pretend you're already thin.

3. Serve plates from the stove or counter in restaurant style. This system requires that you actually get up and go over to the pan to get more instead of simply reaching an arm's length for the second helping.

4. Expansion cooking is great because it provides built-in portion control. People pay dearly for the frozen, ready-to-heat diet dinners that restrict their portions to 300 calories. Why not make your own 300-calorie containers of your favorite meals? One of my favorites is Fantasy Fish (page 171).

5. Tune in while you eat and stop as soon as you're satisfied. The stomach is said to be about the size of a clenched fist—not much food fits in a clenched fist.

6. Keep a large airtight container of ready-to-eat raw vegetables in the refrigerator. Cover the vegetables with cold water and replace the water daily; these crisp, delicious snacks keep well for up to two weeks. If plain, raw vegetables turn you off, try the terrific tasting, fat-free dill dip on page 172.

7. Place a 32-ounce "swig" (the kind you buy at convenience stores for soda) full of water and ice cubes in the fridge before you leave work for the day or before you go to bed at night (if you'll be working at home the following day). The next day you will have a guilt-free, healthy, and cost-effective beverage to carry around and sip as you work. It keeps your mind off food and your stomach from complaining.

8. Next time you are tempted to stop and spend your hard-earned money on something as fattening as burgers and fries, consider opting for one of the many fast-fix entrées offered in chapter 4. Believe me, the last thing you need are the empty, expensive, high-fat foods that await you at the end of that long line!

9. If you are a confirmed chocoholic and have been repeatedly disappointed by so-called "great-tasting" diet desserts, the rich-tasting, Low-Fat Brownie Pie recipe (page 173) and the aforementioned Kiss Delights (page 169) may help you stick with your diet choices. Also, check out Nonfat Chocolate Frozen Yogurt (page 174) and the defatted version of the Chocolate Syrup recipe on page 147. With these nonfat binge-busters, you will have a hard time believing you are not blowing your daily fat allowance.

10. Dieters and penny pinchers can make a low-fat, relatively inexpensive version of peanut butter (page 175). I use this with success in some recipes that call for regular peanut butter, which contains 10 grams fat per tablespoon. But so far I haven't been able to convince my taste buds to eat it on toast.

Kiss Delights

These fat-free morsels are a lifesaver if you crave chocolate but can't afford the fat. The taste reminds me of malted milk balls.

Ingredients	Quantity	2X Quantity
Egg whites	3	6
Cream of tartar	½ teaspoon	1 teaspoon
Sugar	1 cup	1⅔ cups
Cocoa	2 tablespoons	¼ cup
Yield (cookies)	96	180+

Beat egg whites on high until foamy; add the cream of tartar and beat until soft peaks form. Add sugar, 1 tablespoon at a time, beating until stiff peaks form. Fold in the cocoa and drop by teaspoonfuls onto cookie sheets spray-coated or greased. Bake in a preheated 275°F oven for 18 to 20 minutes, until firm but not brown. Cool on baking sheets, then remove and store at room temperature for up to 6 months.

The best news is that each cookie contains only 9 calories and the entire recipe of 96 cookies yields a total of 1½ grams fat. You could eat two-thirds of the recipe before taking in 1 gram of fat.

Defatted Cheddar

If you can find low-fat Cheddar cheese on sale, buy it. If not, here is a way to defat the regular kind.

Cut 4 ounces of Cheddar into ½-inch cubes and place them in a glass bread pan or in a microwave-safe dish of equal size. Barely cover the cheese with tap water, then microwave on high for 3 minutes, stirring after each minute.

Let the substance cool for 10 minutes. Place it in cheesecloth and run it under cold water for 15 seconds (you will *see* the fat coming out!). Press out the excess grease and water.

Defatted Cheddar cheese keeps in the refrigerator for up to 4 days or in the freezer for up to 6 months. Once frozen, cheese must be shredded or crumbled because it will no longer slice.

Note: To avoid a big mess, use cheesecloth. Do not improvise!

Attention dieters: Save 24.6 grams fat per 3½ ounces! 3½ ounces of defatted Cheddar contains 200 calories and 8.8 fat grams compared to 350 calories and 33.4 fat grams for 3½ ounces of regular Cheddar.

Fantasy Fish

Ingredients	Quantity	_X Quantity
Pollock or other fish fillets, thawed	1 pound	
Asparagus spears, cooked	8	
Béchamel sauce (pages 83–84)	1 cup	
Yield	4 servings	

Prepare béchamel sauce according to instructions. Place ½ cup water in a small frying pan and bring to a boil. Meanwhile, pat the fillets dry, sprinkle each with salt and pepper, and lay two asparagus spears in the center of each fillet so that the spears extend from each side. Roll up and seal each with a toothpick. Place into pan with boiling water, reduce heat, and cover. Cook for 5 minutes, or until fish appears opaque. Pour béchamel sauce over the top, cover, and cook until the fish flakes easily with a fork (about 2 minutes longer). Remove fillets, one at a time, to a serving platter; serve hot, or freeze unused portions as individual servings to reheat later in the microwave.

Dill Dip Seasoning Mix

Ingredients	Quantity	_X Quantity
Onion flakes	2 teaspoons	
Dill weed	1 tablespoon	
Spike or seasoning salt	1 teaspoon	
Yield (seasoning mix)	2 tablespoons	

Combine and store indefinitely in a moistureproof, airtight container at room temperature.

Use instructions:

Seasoning mix	2 tablespoons
Sour cream (regular or fat-free)	1 cup
Mayonnaise (regular or fat-free)	1 cup
Yield (dill dip)	2 cups

Combine all ingredients, mix well, and refrigerate for at least 2 hours before serving.

Low-Fat Brownie Pie

You will have a hard time believing that this rich chocolate dessert contains only 2.8 grams of fat per pie!

Dry mix ingredients	Quantity	_X Quantity
Flour	2 cups	
Sugar	⅞ cup	
Cocoa	⅔ cup	
Baking soda	½ teaspoon	
Baking powder	½ teaspoon	
Salt	½ teaspoon	
Yield (dry mix)	3 cups	

Combine all ingredients and store indefinitely in a moistureproof, airtight container at room temperature.

Use instructions:

Dry mix	1 cup
Crème de menthe syrup (page 65)	⅓ cup
Egg white	1
Yield	1 8-inch pie

Preheat oven to 350°F. Spray or grease an 8-inch pie plate. Mix the ingredients until smooth, pour into prepared pie plate, and bake on upper rack for 9 minutes. Cool and frost with peppermint frosting (page 149).

To turn the brownie batter into a chocolate pie crust: Spray or grease two 8-inch pie plates. Mix ingredients until smooth and pour half into each pie plate. Use the back of a spoon to spread batter up sides of the pan. Bake at 350°F for 5 minutes. Allow the crust to cool, then fill with your favorite filling and serve.

Gift suggestion: Give your dieting pal a package of the dry mix with instructions for making the pie and/or pie crusts. It's a losing battle unless we get all the help we can!

Nonfat Frozen Yogurt

Use your heavy-duty kitchen mixer to make this creamy dessert at a price that's half what you'd pay in the supermarket.

Ingredients	Quantity for vanilla	Quantity for chocolate
Liquid nonfat milk	1 cup	1 cup
Vanilla	2 tablespoons	—
Unsweetened cocoa powder	—	⅓ cup
Powdered sugar	½ cup	
Nonfat dry milk powder	1½ cups	1 cup
Egg whites	10	10
Cream of tartar	1 teaspoon	1 teaspoon
Sugar	1 ⅓ cups	1 ⅓ cups
Yield	½ gallon with a total of 94 calories and 0 fat grams per ½-cup serving	½ gallon with a total of 96 calories and 1 fat gram per ½-cup serving

In blender container, combine the first three ingredients for chocolate or the first four ingredients for vanilla. Whir on high for 45 seconds, until smooth. Set aside.

In a large mixing bowl, beat egg whites on high until foamy. Add the cream of tartar and beat until soft peaks form. Gradually add the sugar, 1 tablespoon at a time, until stiff peaks form and then until glossy, about 2 minutes longer. Carefully but thoroughly fold in the blender mixture until cream is of uniform consistency and color. Freeze in an airtight container for a minimum of 6 hours. Serve as ice cream, plain or with toppings.

Better Peanut Butter

You probably already know how fattening and expensive peanut butter is: 100 calories, 10 fat grams, and 15¢ per tablespoon. Try this low-fat, inexpensive version.

1 part peanut butter
to 1 part cooked, mashed carrots or pumpkin

In other words:

1 cup peanut butter + 1 cup cooked, mashed carrots = 2 cups better peanut butter

Refrigerate the mixture for at least 24 hours to allow the flavors to blend. Use within 4 days for best consistency and taste.

12.

The Greatest Source

Congratulations! You've reached the "final frontier." As you begin to employ the tips and recipes in this book, you will find time for more enjoyable activities; you will have money to spend on more lasting items than frozen pizza; and you will (I hope) realize improved health so you can enjoy your family for many years to come.

I've spent many pages sharing ideas that I believe can help reduce the stress in your life, especially in the areas of your time and food budgets. But if I shared my strategies without introducing you to my best friend and greatest Source, this book would be sadly incomplete. No amount of "food freedom" can compare to the peace and security that I have found in knowing God.

A number of years ago I was in an auto accident. As my car spun in front of three lanes of oncoming Minneapolis freeway traffic, I wondered if I would survive. My car was totaled, but I was calm. I knew that even if I died right then, in that spinning car, I had absolutely nothing to fear because my trust in God and in heaven as my future home is complete.

The same God who provided me with peace in that crisis situation still provides me with peace—throughout my daily affairs. Sure, car crashes, job uncertainties, injuries, and other horrible things come into our lives. Yet, while we cannot always trace God's hand, we can always trust His heart.

I am a full-time homemaker trying to keep down the bills without sacrificing my life to food preparation. You may be juggling a career and home responsibilities—just trying to get nutritious food on the table without spending a fortune. Whatever your situation, know that God loves you and offers you peace.

If the overall picture of your life is not "peaceful," consider reading Billy Graham's excellent book, *Peace with God* (Irving, TX: Word Books, 1984) or better yet, read the Bible. It's no accident that the Holy Bible is the best-seller of all time—more solutions are found there than in any other book ever published.

I would love to hear from you. Your questions are welcome, as are your tips and recipes for further streamlining a busy, cost-effective lifestyle. May the God whom I love and serve bless you in every way as you use the resources He has given you more wisely!

13.

Substitutions and Equivalents That Save Time, Money, and Fat Grams

Have you ever realized midrecipe that you were out of cream of chicken soup, evaporated milk, or some other important ingredient? Or have you noticed that many of the recipes in today's cookbooks, magazines, and newspapers call for one or more unusual, expensive, or hard-to-find items? What do you do? A trip to the store is time consuming and often results in your buying more items than you originally intended. Purchasing one "gourmet" ingredient for that fabulous-sounding recipe in last Sunday's magazine section can cost as much as an entire bag of groceries. And surrendering to take-out food—yet again—is a big drain on the budget.

There's no reason to give up on dinner plans or the fun of trying new recipes just because you lack a certain ingredient. By knowing which ingredients can be substituted for which, you can achieve kitchen freedom—and realize tremendous savings. You can also gain more control over the fat content of your diet by learning which low-fat foods can replace the high-fat items.

In the pages that follow, you'll find an A to Z guide to more than four hundred ingredients and foods, from baking powder and baby food to shortening and yogurt. If you don't have a particular item, look it up alphabetically by name and see what you can use as a substitute. If you want to find out if there's a low-fat version of the item in question, look it up and see if I've included a recipe. If the recipe calls for fresh and all you have is dried or frozen, turn to the entry and you can proceed with confidence. If your recipe calls for a pound of apples and all you have are three apples, will you have enough? The answer is, yes, but turn to **Apples** and find out for yourself. Quantity data is included for most items and can help you shop wisely.

While many of the substitutions on the following pages provide equivalent or superior results, some offer suitable second choices and others change the taste of your final product noticeably. All save a trip to the store in a pinch, most save money, and some save fat grams. The following notations will aid you in deciding which substitutions are feasible for your endeavors.

= Equal: Your recipe will turn out the same or better than if you had used the original ingredient.

@ Like: The final product may vary slightly in either taste or texture. This difference may often go completely unnoticed, even by you.

! Emergency: These work but will change the final product noticeably. Please do not assume that it will "ruin" the recipe: it will just be "different" from the recipe you are used to. I often actually prefer these "change-of-pace" outcomes.

> Less Fat: While these change the taste of your recipes slightly, they are honestly "good" substitutes and are worth trying. I have been really excited about the tastes available on a low-fat diet using these options.

$ Less Cost: Almost every substitution listed saves you money. The ones that do not save money are included to save you time in cases where you would have to make a trip to the store if a replacement could not be identified.

"Sugar" refers to white, granulated; "rice" refers to white, long-grain; and "flour" refers to unbleached all-purpose flour, unless otherwise noted. The terms "margarine" and "butter" are used interchangeably.

= Equal   @Like   !Emergency   >Less Fat $Less Cost

Accent

1 teaspoon = 1/16 ounce

1 ounce = 5 tablespoons

Allspice

1 teaspoon = 1/12 ounce

1 ounce = 4 tablespoons

@ equal parts of cinnamon, clove, and nutmeg (juniper berry is included in most allspice mixtures)

Almond frosting

See *Frostings* (page 149).

Anise

1 teaspoon = 1/15 ounce

1 ounce = 5 tablespoons

! tarragon (will alter the final taste but works)

Apples

1 medium apple = 6 ounces

1 pound fresh = 3 medium apples

1 pound fresh = 3 cups sliced or chopped

4 pounds fresh = 1 pound dried

Applesauce

See *Applesauce* (page 105).

Apricots

1 cup = 5 to 13 apricots

5½ pounds fresh = 1 pound dried

1 pound fresh = 8 to 12 whole fresh

1 pound dried = 3¼ cups

1 pound cooked and drained = 3 cups

Arrowroot

See *Thickeners* (page 213).

Avocado

1 = ½ cup mashed

= Equal   @Like   !Emergency   >Less Fat $Less Cost

Baby food

Feeding baby can be simple and inexpensive if you start baby out on the foods your family usually eats. Follow basic guidelines for starting a baby on solids (see any baby care manual or ask your pediatrician). Purée approximately ½ cup of the food you are interested in serving and add water, fruit juice, or broth as follows:

- *Fruits:* ½ cup cooked, mashed fruit plus 3 tablespoons liquid

- *Vegetables:* ½ cup cooked, mashed vegetables plus 3 tablespoons liquid

- *Meat:* ½ cup cooked, mashed meat plus 5 tablespoons liquid (meat broth is fine)

- *Starch:* ½ cup cooked, mashed rice, potatoes, noodles, etc., plus 3 tablespoons liquid

A great advantage to feeding baby a mashed-up version of whatever you're having is that the child becomes acquainted with the foods your family eats instead of with prepared, jarred, expensive baby foods.

Bacon
8 slices = ½ cup cooked and crumbled
1 ounce bacon usually = 1 slice raw bacon
@> turkey bacon (usually a little more expensive)

Bacon bits
1 ounce = ¼ cup cooked and crumbled

Baking powder
1 pound = 2½ cups
1 teaspoon = ⅙ ounce
2½ tablespoons = 1 ounce
1 tablespoon @ ¾ teaspoon baking soda plus 1¾ teaspoons cream of tartar
1 tablespoon @ 2 teaspoons cream of tartar plus 1 teaspoon baking soda plus ½ teaspoon salt plus ½ teaspoon cornstarch

Continued

= Equal   @Like   !Emergency   >Less Fat $Less Cost

Baking powder *(continued)*

1 tablespoon ! when eggs are called for in a recipe and you are out of baking powder, add the egg yolks, reserving the whites. Whip the whites until stiff, then fold in at the end of the recipe; bake as directed. Will create a slightly heavier product.

See also: *Double acting baking powder* (page 193).

Baking soda

1 teaspoon = ⅙ ounce
2 tablespoons = 1 ounce

Bananas

1 pound = 2 large = 5 small
1 medium = 1 cup mashed
1 cup mashed = 14 ounces
1 cup dried = 3⅗ ounce

Basil

1 teaspoon = ¹⁄₂₈ ounce
1 ounce = ½ cup

Bay leaf

1 whole = ¼ teaspoon crushed

Beans

1 cup dried beans = 2 cups cooked
See *Dried Beans* (page 92).

Béarnaise sauce

See *Hollandaise Sauce* (page 109).

Béchamel sauce

See *White Sauce Mix* (page 82).
@ 1 can cream of mushroom soup plus ¼ cup light cream
@ 1 can cream of celery soup plus ¼ cup light cream

Beef

1 pound cooked = 3 cups ground
1 cup pieces = 6 ounces cooked

= Equal   @Like   !Emergency   >Less Fat $Less Cost

Beef broth
See *Broth Mix* (page 75).

Beef consommé
See *Consommé* (page 115).

Beef gravy
See *Gravy Mix* (page 81).

Bisquick
See *Biscuit Mix* (page 79).

Black pepper
1 teaspoon = ⅒ ounce
1 ounce = 3 tablespoons

Blueberries
1 cup = 5¼ ounces

Bouillon
1 teaspoon = ⅒ ounce
1 ounce = 10 teaspoons
Use requirements: 1 to 2 teaspoons + 1 cup water = 1 cup soup
1½ teaspoons bouillon $@ 1 tablespoon soup base
Note: I always substitute "soup base" when a recipe calls for bouillon. It costs less and gives a more natural taste. Many of the mixes included here require chicken, beef, or onion soup base or bouillon. Dry soup bases are sold in 1-pound glass or plastic containers near the bouillon in most supermarkets.

Bran
1 cup = 2 ounces

Brazil nuts
2 pounds in shells = 1 pound shelled
1 pound shelled = 3 cups

Bread
1 pound loaf = 12 to 16 slices
1 slice usually = 1 ounce

= Equal @Like !Emergency >Less Fat $Less Cost

Breading

See *Shake-and-Bake Meat Breading Mix* (page 88).

Bread crumbs

See *Crumbs* (page 192).

Broth

See *Broth Mix* (page 75).

Burger

See *Ground Beef* (page 198) or *Turkey Burger* (page 214).

Butter

1 stick = 4 ounces = 8 tablespoons
4 sticks = 1 pound = 2 cups
$@ margarine
>@ diet margarine
>! Heart Beat spread (cannot be used for frying)
>! Butter Buds (liquid butter replacement)
! Butter Flavored Crisco (see can for instructions)
1 cup ! ⅞ cup clarified bacon drippings
1 cup ! ⅞ cup lard
1 cup ! ⅞ cup oil
1 cup ! 14 tablespoons shortening plus ½ teaspoon salt
1 cup >! ⅜ cup nonfat dry milk plus enough water to yield 1 cup
homemade evaporated skim milk (for use in baking)

Butterscotch chips

12 ounces = 2 cups

Butterscotch sauce

See *Caramel Sauce* (page 146).

Cabbage

1 pound = 4 cups shredded = 2 cups cooked

Cake flour

See *Flour, cake* (page 195).

= Equal   @Like   !Emergency   >Less Fat $Less Cost

Cake mixes

I have tried many recipes for dry cake mix equivalents and have found all to be disappointing in one way or another. When boxed mixes go on sale, I stock up on the flavors we enjoy. If I happen to run out, most recipe books offer numerous "from-scratch" cake recipes that taste marvelous and require only a few minutes' effort.

Caraway

1 teaspoon = $\frac{1}{12}$ ounce
1 ounce = $\frac{1}{4}$ cup
! cumin. Cumin will change the taste, but it works in a pinch.

Cardamom, ground

1 teaspoon = $\frac{1}{16}$ ounce
1 ounce = 5 tablespoons

Carob powder

1 cup = 3 ounces
1 pound = 4 cups
! chocolate. Carob delivers a noticeable taste difference and it's usually more expensive, but it is preferred by some for its "healthful" benefits. Substitute 3 tablespoons carob powder plus 2 tablespoons water for each ounce of chocolate required. Carob is sweeter than unsweetened cocoa, so if you use it to replace unsweetened cocoa, reduce the sugar in the recipe by one-quarter.

Carrots

1 pound = 3 cups shredded = 2½ cups diced

Catsup

1 cup = 10 ounces
1 cup ! 9 ounces tomato sauce plus ½ cup brown sugar plus 2 tablespoons vinegar (for cooking purposes only)

Cayenne

1 teaspoon = $\frac{1}{12}$ ounce
1 ounce = 4 tablespoons
⅛ teaspoon @ few drops Tabasco sauce

= Equal   @Like   !Emergency   >Less Fat $Less Cost

Celery

2 medium stalks = 1 cup diced

Celery flakes

1 teaspoon = ⅟₄₈ ounce
1 ounce = 3 cups

Celery salt

1 teaspoon = ⅛ ounce
1 ounce = 3 tablespoons

Celery seed

1 teaspoon = ⅟₁₂ ounce
1 ounce = 4 tablespoons

Cereals

1 cup flake type = 1 ounce
1 cup granola type = 3½ ounces

Cheese, blue

4 ounces = 1 cup crumbled = Roquefort

Cheese, Cheddar

1 pound = 4 cups shredded
4 ounces = 1 cup shredded
@> *Defatted Cheddar* (page 172)

Cheese, cottage

1 pound = 2 cups
@> nonfat cottage cheese (unfortunately, usually more expensive)
@ ricotta
! feta or cream cheese

Cheese, cream

3 ounces = 6 tablespoons
1 cup !> 4 tablespoons low-fat margarine plus 1 cup nonfat cottage cheese, plus a few drops of liquid nonfat milk: blend on high until smooth.
!> nonfat cream cheese (quite a bit more expensive)
1 cup ! 1 cup plain yogurt

= Equal @Like !Emergency >Less Fat $Less Cost

MARNIE'S KITCHEN SHORTCUTS

Cheese, mozzarella
1 pound = 4 cups shredded
! Monterey Jack

Cheese, Parmesan
1 cup = 3½ ounces
1 pound = 6 cups shredded
@ Romano cheese

Cheese, ricotta
1 pound = 2 cups
! cream cheese
! cottage cheese, blended until smooth

Cheese, Romano
1 pound = 4 cups
@ Parmesan cheese

Cheese sauce
See *White Sauce Mix* (page 82).

Cherries
1 quart fresh = 2 cups pitted
1 pound fresh = about 120 cherries

Cherries, candied
1 cup = 7 ounces

Chicken broth
See *Broth Mix* (page 75).

Chicken consommé
See *Consommé* (page 115).

Chicken gravy
See *Gravy Mix* (page 81).

Chicken meat
Loosely packed . . .
10-ounce breast = 1 cup cooked, deboned, and diced meat
3 pound whole chicken = 3 cups cooked, deboned, and diced meat
4 pound whole chicken = 4½ cups cooked, deboned, and diced meat
5 pound whole chicken = 6 cups cooked, deboned, and diced meat

= Equal @Like !Emergency >Less Fat $Less Cost

Chili powder

1 teaspoon = 1/16 ounce
1 ounce = 5 tablespoons
4 tablespoons @ 3 tablespoons paprika plus 1 tablespoon turmeric plus 1/8 teaspoon cayenne plus 1/8 teaspoon garlic powder
1 tablespoon ! 1 teaspoon each oregano, cayenne, and salt

Chili sauce

1 cup = 8 ounces
1 cup ! 9 ounces tomato sauce plus 1/2 cup sugar (white or brown) plus 2 tablespoons vinegar (for use only in cooking)

Chili without the beans

Follow the **Use instructions** for *Marnie's Favorite Chili Seasoning Mix (After)* on page 68, but add 1 tablespoon cornstarch, eliminate the water, and add no beans. Cook as directed or microwave until heated through, stirring often. This recipe yields about 20 ounces of chili.

Chinese five-spice powder

1 teaspoon = 1/12 ounce
1 ounce = 3 tablespoons
Available from the spice section of your supermarket or from a food co-op.

Chives

1 teaspoon = 1/48 ounce
1 ounce = 3 cups

Chocolate, baking

See *Chocolate, semisweet* or *Chocolate, unsweetened* (page 189).

Chocolate, carob

See *Carob* (page 185).

Chocolate chips

12 ounces = 2 cups
12 ounces melted @ 1 cup cocoa plus 1 1/2 cups sugar plus 1/4 pound margarine, melted, plus 1 tablespoon paraffin

= Equal   @Like   !Emergency   >Less Fat $Less Cost

Chocolate, cocoa, unsweetened

1 cup = 3 ounces
1 pound = 4 cups
1 ounce unsweetened chocolate @ 3 tablespoons unsweetened cocoa plus 1 tablespoon margarine or oil

Chocolate crumbs

See *Crumbs* (page 192).

Chocolate, German

1 square = 1 ounce
4 ounces $@ 3 tablespoons cocoa plus 4½ tablespoons sugar plus 2¾ tablespoons shortening
@semisweet chocolate

Chocolate, grated

1 ounce = 4 tablespoons

Chocolate, mini-chips

2 cups = 12 ounces

Chocolate nonfat frozen yogurt

$@> See *Nonfat Frozen Yogurt* (page 174).

Chocolate, semisweet

1 ounce = 1 square
1 ounce = ⅙ cup chocolate chips
1 ounce $@ 3 tablespoons cocoa plus 1 tablespoon margarine plus 3 tablespoons sugar

Chocolate, unsweetened baking

1 square = 1 ounce
1 ounce = 4 tablespoons grated
1 ounce $@ 3 tablespoons unsweetened cocoa plus 1 tablespoon butter
1 ounce > 3 tablespoons unsweetened cocoa plus 3 tablespoons Butter Buds

Choron sauce

See *Hollandaise Sauce* (page 109).

= Equal   @Like   !Emergency   >Less Fat $Less Cost

Cinnamon

1 teaspoon = $\frac{1}{12}$ ounce

1 ounce = $4\frac{1}{2}$ tablespoons

Citron

1 cup dried, sliced = $6\frac{1}{2}$ ounces

Cloves, ground

1 teaspoon = $\frac{1}{12}$ ounce

1 ounce = 4 tablespoons

Cocoa

See *Chocolate, unsweetened* or *Instant Hot Cocoa Mix* (page 91).

Coconut

1 pound = 6 cups shredded

3 ounces flaked = 1 cup

Coffee

1 pound grounds = 5 cups grounds

3 ounces = 1 cup grounds = 40 cups coffee

$\frac{1}{4}$ cup grounds = 10 cups coffee

Confectioners' sugar

See *Sugar, powdered* (page 212).

Consommé

See *Consommé* (page 115).

Corn

4 ears = 2 cups kernels

Cornmeal

1 pound = 3 cups uncooked

1 pound = 12 cups cooked

1 cup uncooked = $5\frac{1}{2}$ ounces

1 cup uncooked = 4 cups cooked

Cornstarch

1 ounce = 3 tablespoons

1 cup = $5\frac{1}{3}$ ounces

= Equal   @Like   !Emergency   >Less Fat $Less Cost

1 pound = 3 cups
As a thickener: 1 tablespoon thickens 1 cup liquid
1 tablespoon @ 2 tablespoons flour
1 tablespoon @ 4 teaspoons arrowroot
1 tablespoon ! 2 tablespoons peanut butter

Corn syrup

1 cup = 12 ounces
1 cup @ 1 cup honey
1 cup $@ 1 cup sugar plus 2 tablespoons liquid
See also *Oil and Sugar Substitutes* (page 206).

Cranberries

1 cup = 3⅙ ounces uncooked
1 pound = 4 cups
1 pound makes about 3½ cups sauce

Cream, half-and-half

1 cup = 8½ ounces
1 cup @ ½ cup cream plus ½ cup milk
1 cup $@ ⅔ cup nonfat dry milk powder plus 1 cup water

Cream, heavy

1 cup = 8½ ounces
1 cup ! 1 cup whole milk plus ⅓ cup nonfat dry milk powder plus 1
tablespoon oil
1 cup @ ⅔ cup nonfat dry milk powder plus 1 cup whole milk
1 cup @ ⅞ cup milk plus 3 tablespoons butter
1 cup ! ⅔ cup skim milk plus ⅓ cup oil
1 cup ! 1 cup milk plus 3 tablespoons butter

Cream, light

1 cup = 8½ ounces
1 cup ! ⅞ cup milk plus 2 tablespoons butter

Cream of tartar

1 teaspoon = ⅙ ounce
1 ounce = 3 tablespoons

= Equal   @Like   !Emergency   >Less Fat $Less Cost

Cream soup

See *Marnie's "Cream of Anything" Soup Mix* (page 73) and *"Cream of Anything" Vegetarian Soup Mix* (page 74).

Cream, sour

1 cup = 8½ ounces
1 cup ! 1 tablespoon lemon juice plus ⅔ cup nonfat dry milk powder plus water to make 1 cup
1 cup ! 3 tablespoons butter plus ⅞ cup buttermilk or plain yogurt
1 cup @ 1 cup cottage cheese, blended on high until smooth, plus ¼ cup buttermilk
1 cup @ ⅓ cup melted butter plus ¾ cup sour milk

Cream, whipping

1 cup = 2¼ cups whipped
1 cup whipped = 1 cup frozen whipped topping
The ! (emergency substitution) designation on the following options is less than warning enough in this case. These work in a pinch, but should not be expected to taste or act like whipping cream.
1 cup ! ¾ cup milk plus ⅓ cup butter
1 cup ! 1 cup evaporated milk, whipped, plus 2 teaspoons sugar

Croutons

See *Croutons* (page 53).

Crumbs

Use your blender or food processor in short bursts of power to finely crumble any of the following crumb materials. Expensive, pre-boxed options are just what they claim: crumbs! Why pay so much?

Crumbs, bread

1 cup dry = 3 ounces = 4 slices bread
1 cup soft = 2 slices bread
1 cup soft @ ¾ cup cracker crumbs
1 cup soft @ ½ cup dry bread crumbs

Crumbs, cake

1 cup dry = 3 ounces

Crumbs, chocolate wafer

1 cup = 19 wafers = 3 ounces

= Equal   @Like   !Emergency   >Less Fat $Less Cost

Crumbs, corn flake
1 cup = 3 cups whole flakes = 3 ounces

Crumbs, cracker
1 cup = 29 saltines = 3 ounces

Crumbs, graham cracker
1 cup = 13 crackers = 3 ounces

Crumbs, vanilla wafer
1 cup = 22 wafers = 3 ounces

Crushed red pepper flakes
1 teaspoon = $\frac{1}{14}$ ounce
1 ounce = 5 tablespoons

Curry powder
1 teaspoon = $\frac{1}{12}$ ounce
1 ounce = 4 tablespoons

Curry sauce mix
See *White Sauce Mix* (page 83).

Dates
1 pound = 2½ cups chopped
6 ounces whole pitted = 1 cup

Dill seed
1 teaspoon = $\frac{1}{15}$ ounce
1 ounce = $\frac{1}{3}$ cup
! fennel or anise

Dill weed
1 teaspoon = $\frac{1}{26}$ ounce
1 ounce = ½ cup

Double-acting baking powder
1 teaspoon = $\frac{1}{6}$ ounce
1 ounce = 2 tablespoons
1 teaspoon @ 1½ teaspoons single-acting baking powder

= Equal   @Like   !Emergency   >Less Fat $Less Cost

Dressing

See *Oil-and-vinegar dressing* (page 206), *Mayonnaise* (page 108), *Creamy Italian Dressing Mix* (page 76), and *Ranch Dressing Mix* (page 77).

Dry mustard

1 teaspoon = ¼ ounce

1 ounce = 5 tablespoons

1 teaspoon @ 1 tablespoon prepared mustard

Duxelles

$@ You can pay a small fortune for duxelles (mushroom sauce) in the specialty section or you can make up your own for next to nothing on a rear burner while working on another kitchen project. Chop mushrooms to desired size and cook over low heat, stirring occasionally, until reduced by half; store in refrigerator until needed. For a richer flavor, add chopped onion and parsley while cooking.

Egg beaters

¼ cup @ 1 egg

See substitution options below.

Eggs

Jumbo:	4 = 1 cup whole	5 = 1 cup whites	11 = 1 cup yolks
Extra-large:	4 = 1 cup whole	6 = 1 cup whites	12 = 1 cup yolks
Large:	5 = 1 cup whole	7 = 1 cup whites	14 = 1 cup yolks
Medium:	5 = 1 cup whole	8 = 1 cup whites	16 = 1 cup yolks
Small:	6 = 1 cup whole	9 = 1 cup whites	18 = 1 cup yolks

Substitute 1 egg>! 1 heaping tablespoon soy flour plus 1 tablespoon water (for use in baking only).

1 egg >@ ¼ cup egg substitute

1 cup egg whites = 3 cups whipped

Evaporated milk

See *Milk, evaporated* (page 202).

Extracts

1 teaspoon = ⅙ ounce

1 ounce = 2 tablespoons

= Equal   @Like   !Emergency   >Less Fat $Less Cost

Fats, cooking, lard
1 cup = 8 ounces

Fats, liquid
1 cup = 8 ounces

Figs, dried
1 cup = 7 ounces
1 pound = 2⅔ cups chopped

Flour
See specific type or listings under *Thickeners* (page 213).

Flour, barley
1 cup = 4 ounces
Substitute for all-purpose flour 1 cup for 1 cup, up to a maximum of half the flour in the recipe.

Flour, buckwheat
1 cup = 3¾ ounces
Substitute for all-purpose flour 1 cup for 1 cup, up to a maximum of half the flour in the recipe.

Flour, cake
1 cup = 4¼ ounces
1 pound = 4½ cups
@ ⅞ cup all-purpose flour plus 2 tablespoons cornstarch for each cup of cake flour

Flour, cottonseed
1 cup = 5 ounces
Substitute for all-purpose flour 1 cup for 1 cup, up to a maximum of half the flour in the recipe.

Flour, gluten
1 cup = 3½ ounces
Substitute for all-purpose flour 1 cup for 1 cup, up to a maximum of half the flour in the recipe.

Flour, graham

1 pound = 4 cups finely milled
Substitute for all-purpose flour 1 cup for 1 cup, up to a maximum of half the flour in the recipe.

Flour, peanut

1 cup = 4 ounces
Substitute for all-purpose flour 1 cup for 1 cup, up to a maximum of half the flour in the recipe.

Flour, powdered wheat germ

1 cup = 3 ounces
Substitute for all-purpose flour 1 cup for 1 cup, up to a maximum of half the flour in the recipe.

Flour, rice

1 cup = 4½ ounces
Substitute for all-purpose flour 1 cup for 1 cup, up to a maximum of half the flour in the recipe.

Flour, self-rising

1 cup = 5 ounces
8 cups @ 8 cups all-purpose flour plus 5 tablespoons baking powder plus 2 tablespoons sugar plus 1 tablespoon salt

Flour, unbleached white

1 ounce = 4 tablespoons
1 cup = 4¾ ounces
1 pound = 3¾ cups unsifted
1 pound = 4 cups sifted

Flour, whole wheat

1 cup = 3¾ ounces
1 pound = 4 cups unsifted
Substitute for all-purpose flour 1 cup for 1 cup, up to a maximum of half the flour in the recipe.

Frosting

1 pound = 3½ cups
See *Frostings* (page 149).

= Equal   @Like   !Emergency   >Less Fat $Less Cost

Frozen yogurt
See *Nonfat Frozen Yogurt* (page 174).

Garlic, clove
1 clove @ ⅛ teaspoon garlic powder
1 clove @ ⅛ teaspoon garlic salt
1 clove = 1 teaspoon minced garlic

Garlic, crushed
1 teaspoon = ⅛ ounce
1 ounce = 3 tablespoons

Garlic powder
1 teaspoon = ⅛ ounce
1 ounce = 3 tablespoons

Garlic salt
1 teaspoon = ⅛ teaspoon
1 ounce = 3 tablespoons

Gelatin, unflavored
¼-ounce envelope = 2½ teaspoons
2½ teaspoons thickens 1 pint of liquid

German-style chocolate
See *Chocolate, German* (page 189).

Ginger
1 teaspoon ground = 1/12 ounce
1 tablespoon chopped fresh = ⅛ teaspoon ground

Graham crackers
1 pound = 40 squares
1 cup coarse crumbs = 9 squares
1 cup fine crumbs = 11 squares

Grated fruit peel
1 teaspoon fresh peels = ½ teaspoon dried
1 orange = 2 tablespoons zest
1 lemon = 1½ teaspoons zest

= Equal   @Like   !Emergency   >Less Fat $Less Cost

Gravy

See *Gravy Mix* (page 81).

Green onions

9 green onions with tops = 1 sliced onion
5 green onions with tops @ 1 cup chopped

Green pepper

1 medium pepper = 6 ounces = 1 cup diced
1 medium pepper @ 4 tablespoons dried green pepper flakes

Ground beef

1 pound = 2½ cups browned meat
$@> turkey burger

Guacamole

See *Guacamole Seasoning Mix* (page 84).

Ham

1 pound = 2½ cups ground
1 pound = 3 cups cubed
@ turkey ham

Hash browns

4 ounces frozen = ¾ cup
See *Oven Hash Browns* (page 98)

Herbs

1 tablespoon fresh = 1 teaspoon dried
1 teaspoon dried = ¼ teaspoon ground
See entries for specific types of herbs for further details.

Honey

1 cup = 12 ounces
1 cup @ 1 cup corn syrup
1 cup @ 1¼ cups sugar plus increase liquid in recipe by ¼ cup
See also *Oil and sugar substitutes* (page 206).

Horseradish

1 tablespoon fresh grated @ 2 tablespoons bottled

= Equal   @Like   !Emergency   >Less Fat $Less Cost

Hot sauce
See *Tabasco* (page 213).

Italian dressing
See *Creamy Italian Dressing Mix* (page 76).

Italian seasoning
1 teaspoon = ⅛₈ ounce
1 ounce = ½ cup

Jams/jellies
1 cup = 11 ounces

Ketchup
See *Catsup* (page 185).

Kidney beans
1 pound dry = 2½ cups dry
1 pound dry = 6 cups cooked
1 pound can = 2 cups cooked
¾ cup dry beans = 1 pound canned

Kitchen Bouquet
1 tablespoon ! 1 teaspoon caramelized sugar

Lard
1 pound = 2 cups
@ shortening

Lemon
1 pound = 3 to 5 lemons
1 whole lemon = 3 tablespoons juice plus 1½ teaspoons rind

Lemonade
1 cup @ 1 tablespoon lemon juice plus 1½ teaspoons sugar plus
water and ice to equal 1 cup

Lemon frosting
See *Frosting* (page 149).

= Equal   @Like   !Emergency   >Less Fat $Less Cost

Lemon juice

1 ounce = 2 tablespoons
1 teaspoon ! ¾ teaspoon vinegar

Lemon rind

1 ounce = 4 tablespoons
1 lemon = 1½ teaspoons zest
1 teaspoon @ ½ teaspoon lemon extract

Lentils

1 pound = 2½ cups = 5 cups cooked

Lettuce

1 pound = 6 cups bite-size pieces

Lima beans

1 pound dry = 2½ cups = 6 cups cooked

Lipton Onion Soup Mix

1 package = 3 tablespoons
1 package $@ 2 tablespoons onion soup base (see *Bouillon*, page 183).
1 package $@ 1 tablespoon beef or onion bouillon plus 2 tablespoons onion flakes

Low-fat foods

Check under their "high-fat" counterpart name.

Mace, ground

1 teaspoon = ¹⁄₁₂ ounce
1 ounce = 4 tablespoons
! nutmeg

Maltaise sauce

See *Hollandaise Sauce* (page 109).

Maple syrup

See *Maple Syrup* (page 148).

Margarine

1 pound = 2 cups
½ cup = 8 tablespoons = ¼ pound

= Equal   @Like   !Emergency   >Less Fat $Less Cost

⅓ cup = 5 tablespoons
¼ cup = 4 tablespoons
@ butter
! butter-flavored shortening (see can for details)
1 cup ! ⅞ cup oil (for cooking only)
1 tablespoon !> fat-free Butter Buds (not suitable for frying)
1 tablespoon !> 1 teaspoon butter-flavored powder plus increase
liquid in recipe by 1 tablespoon
1 cup !> 7 tablespoons buttermilk powder plus water to equal 1 cup
(for cooking and baking purposes)
1 cup !> 6 tablespoons nonfat dry milk granules plus water to equal
1 cup (for cooking and baking purposes)

Marjoram
1 teaspoon = ⅟₂₈ ounce
1 ounce = ½ cup
@ thyme

Marmalade
1 cup = 11 ounces
! jelly

Marshmallows
1 cup = 13 large
10 ounces = 40 large
1 pound = 64 large = 4 cups
10 ounces = 4 cups mini-marshmallows
1 cup = 25 minis

Marshmallow cream
7-ounce jar ! 10 ounces marshmallows melted with 4 tablespoons
margarine

Mayonnaise
1 cup @> 1 cup Miracle Whip Free plus 2 tablespoons extra liquid
See *Mayonnaise* (page 108).

Meat, ground raw
1 pound = 2 cups raw = 1½ cups cooked

= Equal @Like !Emergency >Less Fat $Less Cost

Milk

1 cup = 8 ounces
@ 4 ounces evaporated milk plus 4 ounces water
@ nonfat, skim, 1%, 2%, or whole
$@ ⅓ cup nonfat dry milk powder plus water to make 1 cup

Milk, almond

1 cup @ 1 cup whole or soy milk

Milk, buttermilk

1 cup @ 5 tablespoons buttermilk powder plus enough water to
make 1 cup
1 cup ! 1 cup milk plus 1 tablespoon vinegar or lemon juice: let stand
5 minutes
1 cup ! 1 cup milk plus 1 teaspoon each baking soda and baking
powder
1 cup ! 1 cup yogurt

Milk, evaporated

12 ounces = 1½ cups
1 cup @ 1 cup light cream
1 cup @ 1 cup half-and-half
1 cup $@ ⅔ cup dry milk granules plus water to equal 1 cup
Reversed: 12 ounces evaporated milk plus 12 ounces water = 3 cups
milk

Milk, evaporated skim

12 ounces = 1½ cups
1 cup $@> ⅔ cup nonfat dry milk powder plus water to equal 1 cup
Reversed: 12 ounces evaporated skim milk plus 12 ounces water = 3
cups skim milk

Milk, nonfat dry milk powder

1 cup reconstituted = 3½ ounces powder = ⅓ cup powder plus water
to equal 1 cup
1 pound = 6⅔ cups dry = 5 quarts reconstituted

Milk, skim

1 cup = 8 ounces
1 cup @ ⅓ cup nonfat dry milk powder plus water to equal 1 cup

= Equal   @Like   !Emergency   >Less Fat $Less Cost

Milk, sour

1 cup = 1 tablespoon vinegar plus milk to equal 1 cup
1 cup ! 1 cup yogurt
1 cup ! 1 cup buttermilk

Milk, soy

1 cup ! 1 cup whole or almond milk

Milk, sweetened condensed

See *Sweetened condensed milk* (page 144).

Milk, whole

1 cup = 8 ounces
1 cup @ ½ cup evaporated milk plus ½ cup water
1 cup @ ⅓ cup nonfat dry milk powder plus 2½ teaspoons butter plus
⅞ cup water
1 cup ! 1 cup buttermilk plus ½ teaspoon baking soda
1 cup ! 1 cup soy or almond milk

Mocha frosting

See *Frosting* (page 149).

Molasses

1 cup = 12 ounces
1 cup @ ¾ cup sugar plus 1 tablespoon extra liquid

Monosodium glutamate

1 teaspoon = ¹⁄₁₆ ounce
1 ounce = 5 tablespoons
@ Accent

Mornay sauce

See *White Sauce Mix* (page 82).

Muffin mix

See *Biscuit Mix* (page 79).

Mushrooms

1 pound fresh = 12-ounce can
1 pound fresh = 3 ounces dried
20 whole = 5 cups sliced

= Equal   @Like   !Emergency   >Less Fat $Less Cost

Mushroom steak sauce

See *Duxelles* (page 194).

Mustard

1 tablespoon prepared @ 1 teaspoon dry

1 tablespoon prepared = 1 teaspoon dry plus 1 tablespoon white vinegar

Nacho chips

1 ounce = 15 chips

1 pound = 15 cups whole

1 pound = 7 cups crushed

Navy beans

1 pound = 2 cups dry = 5 cups cooked

Nonfat dry milk powder

See *Milk, nonfat dry milk powder* (page 202).

Noodles, egg

1 pound = 7 cups cooked

7 ounces = 4 cups cooked

Noodles, lasagne

1 pound = 12 to 24 noodles

12 noodles @ 1 9 by 13 or 2-loaf pan recipes of lasagne

Noodles, macaroni

1 pound = 4½ cups cooked

1 cup raw = 2 cups cooked

Noodles, spaghetti

1 pound = 6 cups cooked

Nutmeg

1 teaspoon = $\frac{1}{11}$ ounce

1 ounce = 4 tablespoons

! mace, cloves, or allspice

Nuts

1 pound in shell = 1 cup nutmeats

1 pound chopped = 3¾ cups

= Equal   @Like   !Emergency   >Less Fat $Less Cost

4 ounces nutmeats = 1 cup chopped
! rolled oats baked at 425°F until crunchy and golden
See specific type

Nuts, almonds

3½ pounds in shell = 1 pound nutmeats
1 pound nutmeats = 3 cups
1 cup whole shelled = 4½ ounces
1 cup slivered = 3½ ounces

Nuts, chestnuts

1½ pounds in shell = 1 pound shelled = 2½ cups nutmeats

Nuts, hazelnuts

2¼ pounds in shell = 1 pound shelled = 3½ cups nutmeats

Nuts, pecans

2½ pounds in shell = 1 pound shelled = 4½ cups unshelled

Nuts, pistachios

1 pound in shell = 2 cups shelled = 3⅔ cups unshelled

Nuts, walnuts

2 pounds in shells = 1 pound shelled
1 pound shelled = 4½ cups halves
1 pound shelled = 3¾ cups pieces

Oatmeal

1 pound = 2⅔ cups raw
1 pound = 8 cups cooked
1 cup raw = 1¾ cups cooked

Oats, rolled

1 pound = 4¾ cups raw
1 cup = 3¾ ounces
1 cup @ ¾ cup flour (in cooking/baking)

Oil

1 ounce = 2 tablespoons
1 cup = 7 ounces
1 cup !> ⅞ cup nonfat dry milk powder plus water to equal 1 cup
1 cup !> 7 tablespoons buttermilk powder plus water to equal 1 cup

= Equal   @Like   !Emergency   >Less Fat $Less Cost

Oil-and-vinegar dressing

$@ 1 part vinegar to 2 parts olive oil

$! 1 part lemon juice to 2 parts olive oil

Oil-and-sugar substitutes

Replace 1¼ cups sugar plus ¼ cup oil with 1 cup honey

Replace 1 cup sugar plus 2 tablespoons oil with 1 cup corn syrup

Olives

15 large pimiento-stuffed = 1 cup sliced

36 medium = 1 cup sliced

48 small = 1 cup sliced

Onions

1 medium = ½ cup diced = ⅓ cup sautéed

1 medium @ 2 tablespoons onion flakes

1 medium @ 2 teaspoons onion powder

1 medium @ 1 teaspoon onion salt and reduce salt in recipe by ½ teaspoon

Onion flakes

1 teaspoon = ¹⁄₁₂ ounce

1 ounce = 4 tablespoons

Onion powder

1 teaspoon = ¹⁄₁₂ ounce

1 ounce = 4 tablespoons

Onion salt

1 teaspoon = ¹⁄₁₀ ounce

1 ounce = 3 tablespoons

Onions, green

9 green onions with tops = 1 cup sliced

Onion soup mix

See *Lipton Onion Soup Mix* (page 200).

Oranges

1 pound = 3 medium

1 medium = 7 tablespoons juice plus 2 tablespoons rind

1 medium = ¾ cup diced

= Equal   @Like   !Emergency   >Less Fat $Less Cost

Orange frosting
See *Frosting* (page 149).

Oregano
1 teaspoon = $\frac{1}{28}$ ounce
1 ounce = $\frac{1}{2}$ cup
! marjoram

Oreo cookie crumbs
1¼ pounds = 6 cups crushed

Pan coating spray
5-ounce can = coating for about 60 9 by 13-inch pans
@ margarine-coated paper towel

Paprika
1 teaspoon = $\frac{1}{14}$ ounce
1 ounce = 5 tablespoons

Parsley
1 bunch = $\frac{1}{2}$ cup chopped

Parsley flakes
1 teaspoon = $\frac{1}{48}$ ounce
1 ounce = 3 cups

Peaches
1 pound fresh = 4 medium
1 pound = 2 cups sliced
5½ ounces dried = 1 cup

Peanut butter
1 ounce = 2 tablespoons

Peanut butter chips
12 ounces = 2 cups

Peanut butter frosting
See *Frosting* (page 149).

Peanuts
1 pound in shells = 3 cups in shells = 1½ cups shelled

= Equal   @Like   !Emergency   >Less Fat $Less Cost

Pears

1 pound fresh = 4 medium
1 pound fresh = 2 cups sliced

Peas

1 pound dry = 2½ cups raw = 6 cups cooked
15 ounce can = 1½ cups peas
1 pound fresh = 3⅓ cups

Pepper

1 teaspoon = ⅒ ounce
1 ounce = 3 tablespoons

Pineapple

8 ounces canned = 1 cup drained

Pistachios

1 pound in shells = 3⅔ cups unshelled = 2 cups shelled

Pizza

See *Pizza Seasoning Mix* (page 86).

Popcorn

2½ pounds kernels = 10 cups kernels
½ cup kernels = 12 cups popped

Poppyseed

1 teaspoon = ⅒ ounce
1 ounce = 3 tablespoons

Potatoes

1 pound = 3 to 4 medium raw
1 pound = 4 cups raw diced or sliced
1 pound = 2¼ cups cooked diced or sliced
1 pound = 2 cups mashed

Potato chips

1 pound = 15 cups
1 pound = 7 cups crushed
4-ounce bag = about 60 chips
@>$ See *Potato Chippers* (page 99).

= Equal   @Like   !Emergency   >Less Fat $Less Cost

Potato, hash browns
See *Hash Browns* (page 198) and *Oven Hash Browns* (page 98).

Potato, instant flakes
1 pound = 16 cups flakes
1 cup flakes = 1½ cups mashed potatoes

Prunes
1 pound dried = 2¼ cups pitted
1 pound cooked and drained = 2 cups

Pudding mixes
I have tried many recipes for dry pudding mix equivalents and have found all to be disappointing in one way or another. When boxed mixes go on sale, I stock up on the flavors we enjoy. If I happen to run out, most recipe books offer numerous "from scratch" pudding recipes that taste great, although all require cooking time.

Pumpkin pie spice
1 teaspoon = ½₂ ounce
1 ounce = 4 tablespoons
1 cup @ ½ cup cinnamon plus ¼ cup ginger plus 2 tablespoons ground cloves plus 2 tablespoons nutmeg

Raisins
1 cup = 5¼ ounces
1 pound = 2½ cups

Ranch dressing
See *Ranch Dressing Mix* (page 77).

Refried beans
1 can = 16 ounces = 2 cups
$= 2 cups cooked, mashed pinto beans plus 3 tablespoons vegetable oil plus 1 tablespoon chili powder plus ½ teaspoon salt: fry over medium-low heat for about 5 minutes.
> 2 cups cooked, mashed pinto beans plus ½ cup Butter Buds plus 1 tablespoon chili powder plus 1 teaspoon salt: fry over medium-high heat for about 5 minutes. Watch carefully to prevent scorching.

= Equal   @Like   !Emergency   >Less Fat $Less Cost

Rhubarb

1 pound = 2 cups cooked

Rice, instant

1 ounce = ⅛ cup dry = ⅔ cup cooked
1 cup raw = 2 cups cooked

Rice, white, regular

1 pound = 2 cups dry = 6 cups cooked
1 cup = 1 cup converted rice
1 cup = 1 cup Minute instant rice

Rice, white, long-grain

1 pound = 2 cups dry = 6 cups cooked

Rice, wild

1 ounce = 3 tablespoons = ½ cup cooked
1 cup = 2⅘ cups cooked
1 pound = 9 cups cooked

Salt

1 teaspoon = ⅙ ounce
1 ounce = 4 teaspoons

Salted crackers

1 pound = 160 squares
1 cup crumbs = 7 squares coarsely crumbled

Sausage

1 pound = 2 cups browned
@> turkey sausage
! ground beef plus a few drops liquid smoke

Scallions

See *Green onions* (page 198).

Shake and bake

See *Shake-and-Bake Meat Breading* (page 88).

Shortening

1 cup = 7 ounces

= Equal   @Like   !Emergency   >Less Fat $Less Cost

1 pound ! ½ pound butter plus 1 cup oil whipped in blender (refrigerate)
1 pound ! 2¼ cups margarine (refrigerate)
1 cup ! ⅞ cup oil
1 cup !> ⅔ cup nonfat dry milk powder plus water to equal 1 cup
1 cup !> 7 tablespoons buttermilk powder plus water to equal 1 cup
!> nonfat yogurt

Shrimp

1 pound small = 50 shrimp
1 pound jumbo = 20 shrimp

Shrimp cocktail sauce

See *Shrimp Cocktail Sauce* (page 51).

Soup bases

1 ounce = 4½ teaspoons
@1 to 1½ teaspoons plus 1 cup water = 1 cup soup
See also *Bouillon* (page 183).

Soy sauce

1 ounce = 2 tablespoons
¼ cup @ 1 teaspoon caramelized sugar plus 1 teaspoon beef bouillon plus 3 tablespoons water
¼ cup @ 3 tablespoons Worcestershire plus 1 tablespoon water

Spaghetti sauce

See *Spaghetti Sauce Seasoning Mix* (page 87).

Spike

1 teaspoon = ⅛ ounce
1 ounce = 3 tablespoons
@ seasoning salt

Stock

1 cup = 8 ounces
Many recipe books offer instructions for assembling rich stock bases including broth from freshly stewed meats and vegetables; when possible, this is ideal. When stock is needed immediately and no fresh broth is available, the following options work:

= Equal   @Like   !Emergency   >Less Fat $Less Cost

Stock *(continued)*
1 cup ! 2 teaspoons bouillon plus 1 cup water
1 cup ! 1 tablespoon soup base (see *Bouillon,* page 183) plus 1 cup
water

Strawberries
1 quart fresh = 4 cups sliced
10 ounces frozen = 1 cup

Sugar
See also *Corn syrup* (page 191), *Honey* (page 198), *Maple Syrup*
(page 148), *Molasses* (page 203), and *Oil-and-sugar substitutes*
(page 206).

Sugar, brown
1 cup = 6 ounces
1 pound = 2½ cups firmly packed
1 pound ! 2¼ cups white sugar
½ cup @ ½ cup granulated sugar plus 1 tablespoon molasses: whir in
blender

Sugar, granulated white
1 pound = 2 cups
1 cup ! 1½ cups molasses plus reduce liquid by 3 tablespoons
1 cup ! 1 cup corn syrup plus reduce other liquid by ¼ cup
2 cups ! 1½ cups maple syrup plus reduce other liquid by ¼ cup
1 cup ! ⅔ cup honey plus ¼ cup flour (or omit flour and reduce liquid
by ¼ cup)
1 cup ! 1 cup brown sugar
1 cup ! 2 cups powdered sugar

Sugar, maple
1 cup = 6 ounces
½ cup @ 1 cup maple syrup plus reduce other liquid by ⅔ cup

Sugar, powdered
1 cup = 5 ounces
1 pound = 3 cups
4 cups @ 2½ cups white sugar whirred in blender until fine

= Equal   @Like   !Emergency   >Less Fat $Less Cost

Sweetened condensed milk
See *Sweetened Condensed Milk* (page 144).

Syrup
See *Corn syrup* (page 191) and *Maple Syrup* (page 148).

Tabasco
1 teaspoon = ⅙ ounce
1 ounce = 2 tablespoons
Few drops of Tabasco @ dash of cayenne
4 drops of Tabasco @ ⅛ teaspoon cayenne

Tacos
See *Taco Seasoning Mix* (page 85).

Tapioca
2 tablespoons quick cooking = 4 tablespoons pearl

Tea
1 pound = (yields) 125 cups

Thickeners
1 tablespoon flour thickens 1 cup liquid
1 tablespoon flour @ ½ tablespoon cornstarch
1 tablespoon flour @ 2 teaspoons arrowroot
1 tablespoon flour @ 1 tablespoon quick-cooking tapioca
1 tablespoon flour @ ½ tablespoon potato flour
1 tablespoon flour ! 1 tablespoon peanut butter
! add mashed potato flakes, a little at a time, stirring constantly until
desired consistency is achieved

Thyme
1 teaspoon = ¹⁄₂₄ ounce
1 ounce = ½ cup
! marjoram

Tomatoes
1 cup canned = 1½ cups whole
1 pound canned whole = 3 medium
1 medium = 1 cup chopped

= Equal   @Like   !Emergency   >Less Fat $Less Cost

Tomatoes (continued)
1 pound = 3 tomatoes
½ cup tomato sauce plus ½ cup water @ 1 cup packed tomatoes, blended
1 cup canned @ 1⅛ cups cut up fresh, simmered 10 minutes

Tomato juice
1 cup = 8 ounces
1 cup ! ½ cup tomato sauce plus ½ cup water

Tomato paste
¾ cup = 6 ounces
6-ounce can plus 1 cup water = 15 ounces tomato sauce
1 tablespoon ! 1 tablespoon catsup

Tomato purée
1 cup = 8 ounces
1 pound 13-ounce can tomatoes @ 15 ounces tomato sauce plus ½ cup water
1 cup @ 2 tablespoons paste plus water to make 1 cup

Tomato sauce
2 cups = 15 ounces
15 ounces = ¾ cup tomato paste plus 1 cup water
15 ounces = 2 pounds cooked, seasoned tomatoes

Tomato soup
1 can = 10¾ ounces
1 can $@ 1 cup tomato sauce plus ¼ cup milk

Tortilla chips
See *Nacho chips* (page 204).

Turkey breast
7 pounds cooked, deboned breast = 12 cups meat plus 3 cups broth @ chicken breast

Turkey burger
1 pound = 2½ cups browned
@ ground beef

= Equal   @Like   !Emergency   >Less Fat $Less Cost

Turkey ham

1 pound = 2½ cups ground
1 pound = 3 cups cubed
@ ham

Turkey, whole

1 pound = 6 ounces cooked, deboned
6 ounces cooked = 1 cup
14 pounds cooked, deboned = 14 cups meat plus 7 cups broth
@ chicken

Unflavored gelatin

¼ ounce envelope = 2½ teaspoons

Unsweetened chocolate

1 square = 1 ounce
1 ounce @ 3 tablespoons cocoa plus 1 tablespoon shortening
1 ounce @ 3 tablespoons carob powder plus 2 tablespoons liquid
plus reduce sugar in recipe by ¼ cup

Unsweetened cocoa

1 cup = 3 ounces
1 pound = 4 cups
1 ounce unsweetened chocolate @ 3 tablespoons plus 1 tablespoon
margarine or oil

Vanilla extract

1 ounce = 2 tablespoons
! almond extract

Vanilla frosting

See *Frosting* (page 149).

Vinegar

1 ounce = 2 tablespoons
1 teaspoon ! 2 teaspoons lemon juice

Wheat allergy flour alternative

1 cup = ½ cup cornstarch plus ½ cup potato, rice, or rye flour plus 2
teaspoons baking powder: sift all together six times.

= Equal   @Like   !Emergency   >Less Fat $Less Cost

Wheat germ
1 cup = 4 ounces

Whipped topping
8 ounces frozen = 2 cups
8 ounces @ 1 cup whipping cream, whipped and sweetened
See also *Cream, whipping* (page 192).

White sauce
See *White Sauce Mix* (page 82).

Wines for marinades
½ cup ! ¼ cup vinegar plus 1 tablespoon sugar plus ¼ cup water (not for use in sauces)

Worcestershire sauce
1 teaspoon = ⅙ ounce
1 ounce = 2 tablespoons
1 tablespoon @ 1 tablespoon soy sauce plus dash of Tabasco

Yeast
1 tablespoon @ ¼ ounce
1 cup = 4 ounces
1 package @ 2½ teaspoons
3.5-ounce yeast cake @ 1 tablespoon active dry yeast

Yogurt
1 cup = 8 ounces
1 cup ! 1 cup buttermilk
1 cup @> 1 cup nonfat yogurt
See *Nonfat Frozen Yogurt* (page 174).

= Equal   @Like   !Emergency   >Less Fat $Less Cost

Appendix I

Handy Charts

Keeping cooking data assembled in one central location is a great way to save time. If you collect helpful cooking charts and information from newspapers and magazines, add a three-ring pocket folder to your Kitchen Notebook and tuck your favorites inside. Be sure to enter the chart titles in the index so you remember where you put them.

The Common Measurements Chart is a handy reference tool. Like the Up-and-Down Chart in Chapter 6, consider making a photocopy of it and taping it to the inside of a kitchen cupboard door for convenient access.

COMMON MEASUREMENTS CHART

⅛ cup	=	2 tablespoons	=	6 teaspoons
¼ cup	=	4 tablespoons	=	12 teaspoons
⅓ cup	=	5 tablespoons + 1 teaspoon	=	16 teaspoons
⅜ cup	=	¼ cup + 2 tablespoons	=	18 teaspoons
½ cup	=	8 tablespoons	=	24 teaspoons
⅔ cup	=	10 tablespoons + 2 teaspoons	=	32 teaspoons
⅝ cup	=	½ cup + 2 tablespoons	=	10 tablespoons
¾ cup	=	12 tablespoons	=	36 teaspoons
⅞ cup	=	¾ cup + 2 tablespoons	=	14 tablespoons
1 cup	=	16 tablespoons	=	48 teaspoons
2 cups	=	1 pint	=	32 tablespoons
4 cups	=	1 quart	=	64 tablespoons

Unlike many baked foods, cakes and brownies require precise cooking times for success. Over- or undercooking a recipe by even 10 minutes may result in unsatisfactory results. Whenever possible, follow a recipe's instructions for time, temperature, and pan size, but if you are rewriting a recipe for a different size pan, the chart on this page will help you determine the correct baking time. Always use the oven temperature given in the original recipe.

All cakes and bars may be baked in a preheated 325°F oven in glass pans or in a 350°F oven in all other types of pans. Unless otherwise noted, grease and flour your pans.

AVERAGE BAKING TIMES FOR VARIOUS PAN SIZES (FOR MOST CAKES AND BROWNIES)

Number of pans	Pan size	Baking time
1	8 by 8-inch	25–30 minutes
1	9 by 9-inch	30–35 minutes
1	9 by 13-inch	35–40 minutes
1	10-inch Bundt	45–55 minutes
2	9-inch rounds	35–40 minutes
2	8-inch rounds	30–35 minutes
3	8-inch rounds	20–25 minutes
8	4-inch cupcakes	30–35 minutes
24	2¾-inch cupcakes	20–25 minutes

The Alternative Pan Size Chart will help you decide if your fancy mold will work for a given recipe, and will provide alternatives if your 9 by 13-inch pan is already in use.

ALTERNATIVE PAN SIZE CHART

When the recipe calls for:	You could use:
4-cup baking dish	9-inch pie plate 8-inch round cake pan small loaf pan
6-cup baking dish	8- or 9-inch round cake pan 10-inch pie plate loaf pan
8-cup baking dish	8-inch square pan 11 by 7-inch casserole loaf pan
10-cup baking dish	9-inch square pan 11 by 7-inch casserole 15 by 10-inch jelly roll pan
12-cup baking dish	13 by 8-inch casserole (up to 12 cups) 13 by 9-inch casserole (up to 15 cups) 14 by 10-inch roasting pan (up to 19 cups)

MOLD VOLUME CHART

Melon mold (7 by 5 by 4 inches) holds 6 cups

8½ by 2¼-inch ring mold (with open center) holds 4½ cups

9¼ by 2¾-inch ring mold (with open center) holds 8 cups

If you live at a high altitude you may already have a conversion chart posted in your kitchen. But just in case you don't, or if you are new to high-altitude cookery, this chart will help you provide great food every time.

HIGH-ALTITUDE COOKING ADJUSTMENTS

FOR ALTITUDES 2,500–4,000 FEET

- Increase baking powder by ¼ teaspoon for each teaspoon recommended.

- Decrease liquid by 1 to 2 tablespoons for each cup required.

- Decrease baking temperature 10 to 15 degrees.

FOR ALTITUDES 4,000–6,000 FEET

- Decrease sugar by ½ teaspoon per cup for each 1,000-foot elevation.

- Use 2 level teaspoons additional flour per cup recommended.

- Decrease baking powder, baking soda, or cream of tartar by ¼ to ½ teaspoon, or use only three-quarters of the amount called for in the recipe.

- Increase liquid by 2 to 3 tablespoons per cup recommended.

FOR ALTITUDES OVER 6,000 FEET

- Decrease sugar by ¼ cup for each cup required.

- Decrease baking powder by ¼ teaspoon for each teaspoon required.

- Increase liquid by 3 tablespoons for each cup recommended.

- Increase baking temperature 10 to 15 degrees.

If you are just getting started in the entertaining business, trying to figure out how much food to make can be a challenge. The following guidelines will help you avoid wasting money. The weights and measurements listed refer to food in its uncooked state. If you are given a range of servings, assume that women and children consume the smaller servings and teenagers and men the larger. Happy hosting!

HOSTESS QUANTITY CHART

Soup as side dish	¾ cup per person
Soup as main dish	1½ cups per person
Fish	4 to 6 ounces per person
Poultry on bone	1 pound per person
Boneless poultry	5 to 8 ounces per person
Beef on bone	6 to 8 ounces per person
Boneless beef	4 to 6 ounces per person
Rice	2 ounces per person
Pasta as side dish	1 ounce per person
Pasta as main dish	2 ounces per person
Vegetables	½ to ¾ cup per person
Lettuce	Large head per 6 people
Dinner rolls	2 per person
Bread as side dish	1 loaf per 10 people
Main dish sauce	2 tablespoons per person
Dessert sauce	2 tablespoons per person
Fruit salad	½ cup per person
Ice cream	¾ to 1 cup per person
Dessert pie	Serves 6 to 8
Two-layer cake	Serves 10 to 12
9 by 13-inch cake	Serves 12 to 16
Cheesecake	Serves 8 to 12
Coffee	2 to 3 cups per coffee drinker

Appendix II

Resources

This appendix features some of the resources that I have found most useful. Many of the most accomplished chefs and home cooks have written books describing their culinary secrets, and these are available to everybody through retail outlets or through a lending library. Your public library may own some of these titles, but even if they do not, there is hope for a free perusal.

Most libraries participate in an interlibrary loan system that has access to thousands of titles. For example, the Warroad Public Library houses a total of about ten thousand volumes, but through the interlibrary loan system patrons have access to more than seven million books! My own practice is to borrow any book I am interested in reading. After having it around for a few weeks, I make a decision on whether it would be useful to have my own copy, or whether it is the type of book I can make a few notes on, return, and never miss. This saves me a lot of money on books—and a lot of space on my kitchen shelves. Next time you're in the market for a good read, check out the following titles:

The American Country Inn and Bed and Breakfast Cookbook, Volumes I and II, by Kitty and Lucian Maynard. (Nashville, TN: Rutledge Hill Press, 1990, 1993).

Never again need breakfast be boring! Invite America's foremost breakfast hosts into your kitchen and the world of great day starters unfolds before your eyes.

Better Homes and Gardens Fix it Fast Cook Book, by the Better Homes & Gardens Staff. (Des Moines, IA: Meredith Corporation, 1979.)

Featuring photos of appetizing meals, all containing four or fewer ingredients, this book is a terrific choice for the busy chef with limited pantry space.

Bonnie's Household Organizer: The Essential Guide for Getting Control of Your Home (revised edition), by Bonnie Runyan McCullough. (New York: St. Martin's Press, 1980.)

By far my favorite home management manual, this 208-page guide by a mother of five provides time, space, and stress-saving tactics that really work.

Cheaper & Better: Homemade Alternatives to Store-Bought Goods, by Nancy Birnes. (New York: HarperCollins, 1988.)

Lots of recipes for everything from barbecue sauce to laundry soap and fly paper.

Diets Don't Work (revised edition), by Bob Schwartz. (Houston, TX: Breakthru Publishing, 1982.)

A refreshing approach to "disconnecting the eating machine" and applying four simple steps to every eating situation. If you have five to fifteen pounds to lose, this is must reading. More than that? Check out *The Underburner's Diet* (page 225).

Fat of the Land, by Fred Powledge. (New York: Simon & Schuster, 1984.)

Startling food facts and buying charts make this book an interesting read.

Great American Food Hoax, by Sidney Margolius. (New York: Walker, 1971.)

A little on the alarmist side, this book does a great job of opening the eyes of processed food buyers to the darker side of convenience. Great tips.

Joy of Cooking, by Irma S. Rombauer and Marion Rombauer Becker. (New York: Scribner, 1995.)

The all-time classic "how and why" cookbook with more than 4,500 recipes and 1,000 illustrations. Explains almost every baffling cooking procedure. This book should be a permanent fixture in every kitchen.

Make Your Own Groceries, by Daphne Metaxas Hartwig. (New York: Macmillan, 1979.)

Everything is made from scratch in this out-of-print treasure chest. It is available through the Minnesota interlibrary loan program; check with your librarian or rare book dealer. It is definitely worth the effort.

Once-a-Month Cooking, by Mimi Wilson and Mary Beth Lagerborg. (Colorado Springs, CO: Focus on the Family Publishing, 1992.)

Mimi and Mary Beth's friendly style and creative system for cooking one month's meals in one day is just the thing if you want to expand on the suggestions in chapter 5.

Reader's Digest Practical Problem Solver: Substitutes, Shortcuts, and Ingenious Solutions for Making Life Easier. (Pleasantville, NY: Reader's Digest Association, 1991.)

For the true do-it-yourselfer, this book is a dream come true. In addition to recipes for potting soil and cat food, it includes loads of other helpful household tips.

Six Ingredients or Less: Cooking Light and Healthy Cookbook, by Carlean Johnson. (Gig Harbor, WA: CJ Books, 1992.)

The combination of advice for low-fat eating with recipes that are quick and easy to prepare makes this spiral-bound recipe collection a real find.

Tightwad Gazette, Volumes I and II, by Amy Dacyczyn. (New York: Villard Books, 1992 and 1995.)

The money-saving tips in these two paperbacks range from practical to outlandish. Ms. Dacyczyn does not mind laughing at her own "tight-waddery," and that makes for very entertaining reading. Many workable suggestions that even the conservative spendthrift could employ.

The Underburner's Diet: How to Rid Your Body of Excess Fat Forever, by Barbara Edelstein, M.D., P.C. (New York: Macmillan Publishing Company, 1987.)

If regular diet plans don't seem to make much of an impression on your figure, take a look at this excellent tongue-in-cheek approach to life as an underburner. I not only enjoy Dr. Edelstein's humor, but also take her suggestions seriously and have experienced success with them when other diets have failed.

Food Information Resources

Books are terrific for many things, but sometimes the only way to really understand a cooking situation is to speak with a home economist or nutritionist. Many companies, organizations, and government offices now provide food information services to their customers. The following list of sources will get you started and you can add to it as you come across others. Soon you will have an arsenal of great minds helping you succeed in every cooking adventure.

One free resource that you may not be aware of is the national directory of toll-free numbers: 1-800-555-1212. The 1-800 information operator at this number will give you the toll-free number for any company you wish to contact, providing they have one. Be sure to have the company name ready when you call. Also remember that nearly every package label lists the manufacturer's name, city, and state, so even if the company does not have an 800 number, you can obtain a local phone number by identifying the area code (look it up in your phone book or call the operator) and then calling information at 1-their area code-555-1212. While 1-800 numbers are free, some areas charge flat fees for information calls. Your operator can tell you more.

American Dairy Association
6300 North River Road
Rosemont, IL 60018
847-803-2000

Helps answer questions about recipes and the use and care of dairy products.

American Egg Board
1460 Renaissance Drive
Park Ridge, IL 60068
847-296-7043

Answers questions on a variety of topics from recipes to nutrition.

American Meat Institute
PO Box 3556
Arlington, VA 20007
703-841-2400

Provides information on safe food handling, meat inspection, nutrition and fat.

American Seafood Institute Hotline
800-EAT-FISH

Open 9 A.M. to 4 P.M. weekdays
Information on how to tell if fish is fresh and how to store and prepare it.

Butter Buds Products
800-231-1123
New York residents call 800-336-0363

Helps fat-conscious cooks substitute this product for margarine and butter. Offers tips and recipes upon request.

Canned Food Information Council
500 North Michigan Avenue, Suite 200
Chicago, IL 60611
312-836-7279

Provides tips and nutrition information, and publishes cookbooks with recipes featuring canned foods.

Consumer Information Catalog
Pueblo, CO 81009
719-948-3334
Written inquiries will be awarded with a catalog listing 200 federal consumer publications from which to choose.

Crisco
800-543-7276
Answers questions regarding its own products.

Dannon
800-321-2174
Answers questions regarding its products; recipes available upon request.

Food and Drug Administration
301-443-1544
Open 8 A.M. to 4:30 P.M. EST weekdays
Answers inquiries regarding new foods and food standards.

Hershey's Chocolate
800-468-1714
Helpful operators assist cooks in making conversions or in using any of its own food products. Recipes and coupons available upon request.

Idaho Potato Commission
PO Box 1068
Boise, ID 83701
Offers *The Idaho Potato Microwave Cookbook* to consumers who send a self-addressed stamped envelope.

Kraft Foods
800-431-1001
Answers questions about its products.

Meat & Poultry Hotline
U.S. Department of Agriculture
Room 1165, South Building
Washington, DC 20250
800-535-4555
202-472-4485

Answers questions about wholesomeness, storage, and labeling of meat and poultry products.

National Frozen Food Association
PO Box 398
Hershey, PA 12033
717-657-8601

Offers information on frozen foods.

Nutrition Action Newsletter
1755 S Street NW
Washington, DC 20009
202-332-9110

Provides data regarding food content and hazards, the food industry, and government regulation of food.

Office of Government and Public Affairs
U.S. Department of Agriculture
Washington, DC 20250
202-205-0027

Provides information on all USDA programs, including publications available for free or minimal charge.

Pillsbury Company
2866 Pillsbury Center
Minneapolis, MN 55402
800-767-4466

Answers questions about its products.

Polly-O Dairy Products
800-845-3733

Operators can tell you where you can buy their low-fat and nonfat cheeses. Recipes available upon request.

Promise Ultra Fat Free Margarine
800-735-3554

Call to learn where you can buy this fat-free product.

SACO
800-373-7226

Helpful information regarding using low-fat buttermilk powder as a replacement for high-fat, high-cost, dairy-case buttermilk.

United Fresh Fruit and Vegetable Association
727 North Washington St.
Alexandria, VA 22314
703-836-3410

Provides information on the nutritional value, seasonal availability, care, and preservation of fruits and vegetables.

Index of Ingredients

(excluding the staple ingredients: flour, sugar, salt, and pepper)

Accent, 120
Allspice, 89, 156
Almond extract, 149
Almonds, 30
Apples, 105
Asparagus, 171
Avocado, 84

Baking powder, 66, 70, 79, 132, 173
Baking soda, 57, 110, 157, 173
Bananas, 55, 58, 106
Basil, 53, 86, 88, 127
Beans, 92, 93
Beef, 88, 129
   see also Ground beef
Black beans, 92
Black-eyed peas, 92
Bouillon
   beef, 35, 75, 81, 115, 124
   chicken, 30, 54, 73, 81, 115, 124
   onion, 90
   vegetable, 74
Bread, 53, 54, 120, 126
   dough, 52
   crumbs, dry, 35, 88, 90
Broth, 83

Brown sugar, 57, 118, 130, 132, 146, 148, 157, 158
Butter, 62, 66, 100, 107, 161
   see also Margarine

Cabbage, 78, 121
Caramel topping, 56
Carrots, 100, 175
Catsup, 51, 90, 125, 130
Cayenne, 68, 84
Celery, 123, 124
   flakes, 54, 73
   salt, 53, 73, 78, 88
   soup, 73
Cheese
   Cheddar, 27, 45, 82, 107, 117, 129, 170
   cottage, 46, 107, 129
   cream, 103, 152
   mozzarella, 129
   Parmesan, 31, 46, 53, 83, 102, 127, 129
Chicken, 29, 47, 88, 123, 124
Chickpeas, 92
Chili powder, 67, 68, 85, 130
Chives, dried, 81
Chocolate
   bark, 160
   chips, 57, 62, 145, 159
   cookies, cream-filled, 56
   frosting, 154

Index

Black-eyed peas, 92
Black pepper, equivalents, 183
Blueberries, equivalents, 183
Blue cheese, equivalents, 186
Bon Appetit magazine, 113
Bonnie's Household Organizer, 22, 223
Bouillon, 183
Bran, equivalents, 183
Brand names vs. generics, 14
Brazil nuts, equivalents, 183
Bread
    crumbs, equivalents, 192
    defrosting in microwave, 26
    equivalents, 183
    French or Italian loaves, 155
    frozen, 143
    honey wheat, 150
    quantity to serve, 221
    see also biscuits and rolls
Breakfast options, 15
    croissants, 153–154
    granola, 158
    pancakes, 80
    waffles, 80
Broth
    low-fat and low-sodium, 165
    mix, 75
Brownie
    mix, dry, 63
    pie, low-fat, 173
Brown 'n' serve rolls, 152
Brown sugar
    equivalents, 212
    softening, 25
Bouillon, 183
Bulk buying, 8–10
Burritos, 116
Butter
    flavored shortening, 63
    equivalents, 184
    Italian, 126
    softening in microwave, 25
    substitutions, 184
Buttermilk
    equivalents, 202
    powder, as fat substitute, 164
Butterscotch
    chips, 184
    sauce, *see* Caramel sauce

Cabbage, equivalents, 184
Cake
    crumbs, equivalents, 192
    flour, equivalents, 195
    mixes, 185
    quantity to serve, 221
Calorie free, definition, 163
Candy
    fudge, 145
    mounds bars, 159
    peanut butter cups, 160
    tootsie rolls, 161
Canned fruits and vegetables, 96–97
Canola oil, 164
Caramel sauce, 146
Caraway seed, equivalents, 185
Cardamom, ground, equivalents, 185
Carob powder
    equivalents, 185
    as substitute for chocolate, 185
Carrots, equivalents, 185
Casserole dishes
    in quantity, 39–40
    reheating from frozen, 40
Catsup
    equivalents, 185
    as substitute for tomato sauce, 185
Cayenne, equivalents, 185
Celery
    equivalents, 186
    flakes, 186
    salt, 186
    seed, 186
Cereal
    granola, 158
    high cost of, 15
Chapian, Marie, 162
Cheaper and Better: Homemade Alternatives to Store-Bought Goods, 223
Cheddar cheese
    defatted, 170
    equivalents, 186
    freezing, 40
Cheese
    comparison pricing, 9
    fat-free, 165
    loaf, 126
    sauce, 82

mounds bars, 159
peanut butter cups, 160
poppycock, 157
sugar and spice nuts, 156
tootsie rolls, 161
Honey
equivalents, 198
syrup, 103
Honey wheat bread, 150
Horseradish, equivalents, 198
Hostess quantity chart, 221

Ice cream
quantity to serve, 221
toppings, 65, 146, 147, 148
see also Frozen yogurt
Ice cube trays
for broth, 165
for pesto, 127
Incredible fried fish, 49
Italian or French loaves, 155
Italian dishes
cheese loaf, 126
deep-dish pizza dough, 128
lasagne, 129
pesto, 127
pizza, 32, 34, 50, 86
spaghetti pie, 46
Italian seasoning, equivalents,
199

Jams and jellies, equivalents, 199
Johnson, Carlean, 26, 224
Joy of Cooking, 223

Kidney beans, 92
equivalents, 199
Kiss delights, 169
Kitchen Bouquet, equivalents, 199
Kitchen efficiency, 22–35
bulletin board, 6
cleanup, 23
microwave, 23–26
nine time-saving recipes, 27–35
organization, 22–23

utensils, 23
Kitchen notebook, 4–5
daily food diary, 11
master price list, 7–8
master shopping list, 6–7
personalizing, 11–12
recipe roster, 10–11

Labels
for dry mixes, 60
for freezer, 38
Lagerborg, Mary Beth, 224
Lard, equivalents, 195, 199
Lasagne, 129
equivalents, 204
Layered tamale pie, 45
in quantity, 39
Layered turkey bake, 47
in quantity, 40
Leftover meats
barbecues, 131
chow mein, 123
refrigerator biscuits, 32
turkey rice pilaf, 30
turkey salsa quickies, 27
yorkshire strata, 28
Lemon
equivalents, 199–200
frosting, 149
Lemonade, equivalents, 199
Lentils, 92
equivalents, 200
Lettuce, quantity to serve, 221
Light, definition, 163
Lima beans, 92
equivalents, 200
Lipton onion soup mix, equivalents,
200
Low fat, definition, 163
Low-fat tips and recipes, 163–177
better peanut butter, 175
brownie pie, 173
defatted Cheddar, 170
dill dip seasoning mix, 172
fantasy fish, 171
kiss delights, 169
frozen yogurt, 174

About the Author

Marnie Swedberg grew up in Minneapolis, Minnesota, where she took over her health club class after her instructor failed to show up one day. From this early start, at the age of sixteen, she went on to health club management and later branched out to provide corporate fitness programs. This management experience as well as interest in health and fitness contributes to the ideas found in *Marnie's Kitchen Shortcuts*.

Currently residing in Warroad, Minnesota, Marnie provides home schooling for her three children, serves as president of the local Friends of the Library, leads a latch-key girls club and local AWANA club, and pursues many other small town activities and interests. In order to find time for community involvement and for more rewarding relationships with her family and friends, she developed the hundreds of shortcuts detailed in this book. These secrets will help you find time in your busy schedule, time that you can use to invest in the relationships in your life.